Maskwork

by Jennifer Foreman

with photographs by
Richard Penton

HEINEMANN
Portsmouth, NH

Heinemann
A division of Reed Elsevier Inc.
361 Hanover Street
Portsmouth, NH 03801-3912
http://www.heinemanndrama.com
Offices and agents throughout the world

First Published in the USA by Heinemann
First Published in the U. K. by The Lutterworth Press
ISBN 0 325 00167 7

Book and cover design: Richard Penton
Electronic typesetting: Bob Allison
Set in Monotype Bembo and Monotype Gill Sans.

This edition published by arrangement with The Lutterworth Press.

Foreman, Jennifer.
    Maskwork / by Jennifer Foreman: with photographs by Richard Penton.
        p. cm.
    ISBN 0-325-00167-7
    1. Mask making   2. Masks.   I. Title.
TT898.F66 1999
745.59--dc21   99-35439

Printed in Hong Kong by **Dah Hua**

Glossary

A3 an international paper size measuring 297 x 420mm or 11¾ x 16½ inches.

A4 an international paper size measuring 210 x 297mm or 8¼ x 11¾ inches.

Brown paper gum-strip a gummed paper packaging tape, which can be purchased in rolls from post offices and stationers.

Das a self-hardening clay widely available from art, craft, toy shops and educational suppliers.

Fibreglass glass fibres mixed with epoxy resin which hardens to a durable, lightweight finish. Small amounts can be purchased from boat builders and model-making shops.

Mod-Roc or **Gypsona** a fabric reinforced plaster used in model-making and plaster cast making. Packets are available from art and craft shops or medical suppliers.

Papier-mâché paper pulp or pieces of paper used with adhesives to mould into shapes. It can be home-made or purchased from educational suppliers, model-making, craft and art shops.

Plasticine a pliant material widely used for model-making. It comes in many colours and is obtainable from art, craft, toy shops and educational suppliers.

Plaster of Paris a fine powder of gypsum, used for making plaster casts etc. It is obtainable from educational suppliers, model-making, craft and art shops.

Play Doh a soft modelling material obtainable from craft or toy shops.

Play dough a home-made version of **Play Doh**. Mix together equal parts of plain flour and salt with enough water to make pastry. Keep in an airtight container in a refrigerator.

P.V.A. a water based adhesive suitable for general use and providing a protective finish.

Contents

* Denotes an entry in the glossary.

Prologue

'Will anyone turn up?' was the question on my mind. It was seven o'clock on a cold October evening. The small room, above the back of the empty theatre, was dark and seemed even colder than outside. 'It is a pity,' I told myself, 'that the room was so difficult to find.' I began to unpack my collection of scissors, paper, gum-strip and card. I tried putting the jumble of small tables and chairs into some kind of order. Leaflets about the evening class had been distributed, and six people had signed up. 'I'll give it another ten minutes,' I said to myself, then I heard voices say, 'Is this the mask workshop?' Three beaming faces appeared from nowhere and I was in business.

It was Jane Thomas who asked me if I had 'any ideas' for her programme of evening workshops at Spring Street Theatre. At last I had an opportunity to explore my enthusiasm for masks and theatre, originally sparked by John Harris when I joined his mask seminars as an undergraduate at Hull University's Drama Department. The mask workshops I offered proved to be popular and attracted students, teachers and everyone locally, or so it seemed, with a passion for theatre who wished to learn something different. The workshops grew when Helen Wragg included me in her 'Summer in the City' dance project. Pam Dellar's invitation to 'help her out' with a few evening classes resulted in a full-scale mask and costume performance. I would like to thank all four for giving me so many opportunities to develop my ideas in those early days.

The chance to research for this book and so share my enthusiasm for learning more about masks with even more people, came after I spotted an advertisement in 'The Independent' newspaper for the BEROL/NSEAD 1989 Curriculum Development Award, (Berol being the pen makers and NSEAD being the National Society for Education in Art and Design). The bursary enabled me to begin this book and I am greatly indebted to John Steers, General Secretary of NSEAD, for his faith in *Maskwork* as a viable publication.

Over the years there have been many other people who have contributed to the evolution of this book. I would like to thank the LEA advisers in the late 1980's at Humberside County Council (as it used to be) for enabling me to run workshops in local schools, as part of 'The Arts in Schools Project' and for permission to reproduce photographs of workshops at these schools: Grange First School,

Grimsby; Headlands School, Bridlington; Keyingham School, Keyingham; Newland School for Girls, Hull; St. Nicholas School, Beverley; Tweendykes Special School, Hull; Winifred Holtby School, Hull; Withernsea High School, Withernsea. I would like to thank the teachers and pupils at these schools for their participation.

I wish to acknowledge the assistance of staff in the Education Department of the British Museum and Students' Room at the Museum of Mankind. Thanks are also due to the Department of Greek and Roman Antiquities, the Egyptian Department and the Department of Oriental Studies at the British Museum, and to the staff of the Horniman Museum.

I would like to thank Professor Nick Stanley for his advice on the ethnographic subject matter and Dr. James Booth for his patient help with the text. Sue McIntyre is thanked for proofreading the book. Andrew Greensmith, and the staff at Kall Kwik, Hull, perfected the laser copies, and thanks are given accordingly. Thanks are due to Professor Jenkins of Harvard University for permission to quote from one of his articles, free of charge. I wish to thank Adrian Brink, Colin Lester and staff at The Lutterworth Press. They have been a source of encouragement and advice. Also, Kate and Christophe Grillet are thanked for their generous hospitality on my frequent trips to Cambridge.

Special thanks are due to my family for allowing me the time to work. In particular, my two daughters who have, literally, grown up with the book.

Finally, I would like to acknowledge both Richard Penton and Bob Allison. I am greatly indebted to Bob for generously giving his time and skill in setting out the whole book on computer and for his impeccable advice and good humour throughout.

Richard collaborated closely with me on this book from manuscript through to publication, and undertook the photography of people maskmaking in addition to most of the unique mask material which he also helped to track down. Eventually he took over the management of the manuscript from its first stages through to designing the layout of the text and photographs, as well as organizing all the photographic permissions and the comprehensive index. It has been a lengthy undertaking and I am greatly indebted to him; without his commitment *Maskwork* would not have been possible.

Front Cover. 'Sun God', from Raven mask-making workshop. *Designed and worn by a student at Winifred Holtby School, Hull. 1989.*
Back Cover. 'Princess Sita', heroine of the *Ramayana* epic. Carved wood. *Balinese. Private collection. 20th century.*
Frontispiece. 'The Politician', full-face character mask made from a moulded brown paper gum-strip base with ears and nose modelled in card. *Designed and worn by a student in the author's mask-making workshop, Hull Dance Project, Spring Street Theatre. 1989.*

Acknowledgements of Photographs

Out of one hundred and eighty two photographs in this book, twenty three are from outside sources:

a. We are indebted to the following owners for generously loaning their pictures without charge: Bob Allison, 150–157; the Bulgarian Museum of Ethnology, Sofia, 12; Vivienne Gardner, 159; Jocelyn Herbert, 27, 170; Professor Mary Miller, Yale University, 15; Staatliche Museen, Berlin, 44; and Trestle Theatre Company, 28, 138.

b. Reproduced by permission of the British Museum, 91.

c. The photographs of the following copyright owners are acknowledged with thanks: Sue Jenkinson, 27, 170; Steve Morgan, 43. However, despite every effort, it has not been possible to find these owners and so they are invited to contact The Lutterworth Press.

We are grateful to Hans De Marez Oyens for tracking down the source of figure 44.

All the other one hundred and fifty nine photographs are by Richard Penton. Also, thanks are due to the following institutions, private collectors and artists for permission to photograph masks in their collections, free of charge: the British Museum, 9, 11, 14, 16, 21, 22; Cambridge University Museum of Archaeology & Anthropology, 10, 61, 97; Japanese Gallery, Kensington, London, 19, 20, 41; Museum voor Volkenkunde, Rotterdam, 13, 38, 39, 166, 167; Gordon Reece Gallery, Knaresborough, 34; Rijksmuseum voor Volkenkunde, Leiden, 29, 36, 161; Tropenmuseum, Amsterdam, 46; Volkenkundig Museum, 'Gerardus van der Leeuw', Groningen, 37; the Chinese Community, Hull, 158; Lesley Croome, 171; Pär Gustafsson, 168; Polly Richards, 17, 18, 165; Miranda Gray, Artist, 177; Walter Storey, Artist, 171.

Thanks are due to both Bob Allison and Richmond & Rigg, Hull for the high standards with which they processed and printed the photographs.

All images are copyright to the above owners, institutions, artists and photographers.

Introduction

This book explores the creative and educational potential of masks and their life-enhancing properties as a means of communication. There is ample scope for people of all ages to enjoy constructing masks of their own and exploring them through language, drama, dance, mime, movement and music *(figs. 1–2)*. All the ideas and activities are tried, tested and workable, having been used and modified over the years in many different situations.

The mask-making processes outlined in Projects 1 to 6 use paper-construction and brown paper gum-strip techniques, adaptable for the classroom and non-specialist workshop *(figs. 3–5)*. Projects 7 to 8 go on to explore more specialized methods. The process of making is explored from the design stage through to practical use. The aim is to stimulate

Fig. 1 *(facing page)*. Helmet-mask made from papier-mâché and topped with a cylindrical hat adorned with tissue paper flowers, on parade at the Notting Hill Carnival, London, in 1992. This mask is reminiscent of the North Tyrolean carnival masks.

Fig. 2. Children and adults at an open-air paper mask-making workshop, led by the author. *York Early Music Festival. Summer 1987.*

ingenuity in the full imaginative use of materials and the exploration of the principles of design.

Each chapter on mask-making provides vital information and theory in addition to practical, topic-based advice. This means that the reader can be assured that practice is underpinned by theory and knowledge. Whenever masks from different cultures are cited, information to set them within their cultural context is given. In projects 1 to 6, step-by-step mask-making processes are outlined, but there is scope for the reader to develop his or her own solutions to practical problems. Each project has extension activities at differing levels of complexity for exploring the meaning and imagery of the masks once they are made, through expressive arts activities. Where appropriate, there are suggestions for further reading and additional sources of ideas.

The chapter 'Masks and Resources' outlines some of the important arguments surrounding the whole ethical issue of using artefacts from other cultures as resources for our own creative work. Masks make exciting visual stimuli, but it would be irrelevant to bring a set of ready-made masks for groups to use, largely because they will have no point of reference for understanding them. In such instances their response might very well be to fool around and make fun of the masks. Clearly there is some point in introducing masks from other traditions to drama students or in an actor's training; but with young people the main value of maskwork is in what they learn from the process of making their own mask and by devising their own project. Even then we should be aware that there might be a limit to what can be achieved.

As someone trained in both Theatre and Education, I have long recognized that masks have a value in the training of actors and in the art of performance. I have also been aware that their potential as a means of personal expression or educational resource has hardly been recognized. The approach described in this book originated, therefore, as an extension of my theatre training and from a desire to formulate techniques and ideas that could be utilized within the classroom at all levels of education, or at home, or in the studio.

At this point it is worth mentioning some of the superstition that surrounds the effect of wearing masks. Admittedly some people have reservations about the wearing of masks because, it is rumoured, they unleash 'uncontrollable' powers in the wearer. It is true that, in general in our society, masks are debased and often have associations with the 'darker' side of human nature, but this has more to do with the wearer's intentions than with the properties of the mask itself. It is a fact nevertheless, that in much ethnographic literature, unique psychological states are reported in conjunction with the wearing of masks. For example, people are described as 'becoming' the spirits, the dead or whatever the mask was meant to represent. It is, however, impossi-

Fig. 3. Scene from Japanese Noh in performance.

ble scientifically to verify such mental conditions as distinct psychological states.[1]

Moreover, the belief that traditional masked celebrations act as a release for emotional or irrational behaviour is based on false assumptions. Although the mask might very well represent some demon of antisocial behaviour, more knowledge of traditional mask ceremonies reveals that the wearing of the mask is surrounded by restriction, convention and taboo. Society stipulates exactly who should wear what kind of mask and only members of a certain lineage, of a specified age or sex, or with a special quality, may don a particular mask. The privilege of the mask rests upon subtle notions of style and timing.[2] Society harnesses the power of masking for its own ends. These might be cathartic: to heal, to inform or to castigate, but such ceremonies are not a free-for-all.

Wearing a mask for theatrical performance is an exacting discipline.

Fig. 4. 'Bird Man' wears a mask constructed from paper and card and worn like a hat. *York Early Music Festival. Summer 1987.*

For example, the training of actors in Bali and Japan, where a tradition of masked theatre is maintained, is both long and arduous. Even in Japan it is an art associated with the old order and demands formality, constriction and tradition.[3]

Mask theatre demands great sacrifices from the performers; their challenge is to make the wooden mask move as if it were alive. When on stage the actor must reflect the mask but also remain separate from it in order to maximize its presence, keep time and synchronize with the action on stage *(fig. 3).*[4] To perform without conscious mastery of this art would render the mask meaningless and the effect would be not so much damaging as cheapening.[5]

Those using this book will look at what is offered and judge their own starting points, depending upon the ages, interests and abilities of the groups with which they are working. I have used these ideas with groups in England at all key stages of the National Curriculum, ranging from pre-school children through to students in advanced classes. I have also used them with community theatre groups involving people of all ages and for my own work in the theatre.

Fig. 5 *(facing page).* 'Neptune and his Helper'. Neptune wears a mask made from green and silver painted Mod-Roc with cloth hair. *York Early Music Festival. Summer 1987.*

The projects can be adapted and incorporated into particular

Fig. 6 *(top left)*. Mask made from recycled materials, designed and worn by an under-graduate student. *Workshop, led by Andy Earl, Hull School of Architecture. September 1996.*

Fig. 7 *(bottom left)*. Shell mask in production of 'Ocean World'. *Designed in a workshop led by Anita Latham and worn by a student at Newland School for Girls, Hull. 1994.*

Fig. 8 *(right)*. Cardboard mask made for a disabled Colombian man by his children. *Street carnival, Karlskrone, Sweden. Summer 1991.*

modules within Art and Design courses, or Drama, Expressive Arts, Theatre and Performing Arts courses. Mask-making lends itself to strategies designed to forge natural links between a whole range of Craft, Design and Technology modules and English, Drama, Dance, Music, Mime and Movement activities. Projects could be devised for basic Mathematics; others could be useful in Geography, Sociology and Religious Studies. There is limitless scope in mask-making for those planning large-scale group events, when communities come together for festivals, carnivals, parties or fund-raising events *(figs. 4–8)*.

16

What are Masks?

In the West, masks are generally undervalued and misunderstood. For most of us they are party objects, decorations or grotesques to be brought out for a lark at Hallowe'en. A modern-day mask culture has been developed by the film and television industry, particularly in Britain and the United States. We see this reflected in the late Jim Henson's creations and the sometimes superb monsters of special-effects film-making. Sadly, however, in real life we are familiar with masks merely as a means of disguise, often used in criminal acts in order to intimidate. Their worldwide significance as a primary means of human expression and communication is largely ignored. In contrast, in many cultures across the rest of the world, masks are closely linked to all aspects of daily life, often embodying significances which date back many centuries but which are still valued today *(fig. 12)*.

On an individual and personal level a mask is, quite literally, a new face, and as such it can protect, disguise or identify the wearer. Throughout history masks have been made for these three functions.

Fig. 9 (*above*). Roman bronze mask, such masks are generally said to represent an Amazon. Worn by men as parade armour and made to represent mythological beings. *Roman, 2nd century A.D. British Museum, London.*

Fig. 10 (*left*). Samurai mask and helmet from Japan. *Lacquered iron. Cambridge University Museum of Archaeology and Anthropology.*

Fig. 11 *(below)*. Replica of the Anglo-Saxon warrior's helmet and protective face-mask decorated with scenes of fighting found in the burial site at Sutton Hoo, Suffolk, in 1939. The original may have been made for King Raedwald (died 624 or 625). *Iron covered with tinned bronze decorative plates to give a silvered effect. British Museum, London.*

Fig. 12 *(right)*. Full-face mask, headdress and costume of the Koukeri (mummers) of Central and Eastern Bulgaria. The masks are made of fur, cardboard, cloth or wood. They are decorated with seeds, feathers, sequins, glass, mirrors and buttons worked into a face to represent wild beasts. They often have horns and long beards. The Koukeri are men and appear on the first Sunday before Lent, when Winter turns to Spring. The masks are very popular; each village has its own style and tries to outdo the others. *Bulgarian Museum of Ethnography, Sofia. 20th century.*

Fig. 13 *(facing page)*. The mask of Purdah. *Museum voor Volkenkunde, Rotterdam. 20th century.*

Fig. 14 *(facing page)*. Plaster mask of a woman from an Egyptian tomb. Such masks were placed over the mummy head of the deceased. They were not individual likenesses but were moulded from plaster and mass-produced in order to represent stereotypes such as old men, young women, etc. This example is probably from Meir in Middle Egypt and dates from the 2nd century A.D. *British Museum, London.*

In modern times the welder, diver, space traveller, motor cyclist, nurse and skier wear protective masks. In the past such masks have taken the shape of face guards to protect the warrior in battle and to terrify the opponent *(figs. 9–11)*.

The ultimate form of disguise is the 'face-less' mask, which is worn in an attempt to be 'invisible'. Paradoxically, such masks can be said to reveal as well as conceal. The act of wearing a 'face-less' mask often broadcasts the intent and even the status of the wearer *(fig. 13)*. Most masks, however, take the form of a face or features and so give the wearer an identity. Why this should be so is a complex and fascinating question. A special regard for both face and head is seen in many cultures and throughout many historical periods.[1] For example, the head-hunters of Borneo chopped off the head of the enemy in the belief that this conquered the spirit living behind the face. The head itself was preserved and treasured. This belief in spirits residing behind the face may have led the earliest peoples to represent their gods in facial images such as masks.[2]

Again, the importance of the face is evident in the lengths to which many early civilisations went in order to preserve the facial image (and so the spirit) of their dead *(fig. 14)*.[3] In ancient Egypt, facial 'masks' were made of painted cartonnage (linen bandages which were soaked in resin and covered with plaster) for the process of mummification, but in Pre-Hispanic Mexico they were made from semi-precious stones and precious metals.[4] There is no evidence to suggest, however, that these masks were used for anything other than covering the faces of the deceased, presumably so that their spirit could recognize them in the afterlife.[5]

Masks made to be worn have far more to do with life and our experience of living than with death. In life, the face is our primary means of recognition and identification. By putting on a face mask we conceal our personal identity and take on that of another. The major significance of the mask lies not, however, in the simple fact of concealment, but in the complex ideas surrounding the question of the new identity or face, and what it represents. The very fact that a new identity can be adopted opens up the limitless human potential of make-believe.[6] The observer can appreciate the meaning of the mask on many levels. Those outside the culture or with no understanding whatsoever of the mask's iconography may receive only confused impressions. The meaning of the mask may be lost even to the community in which it was created, but it may still be considered important. Another mask may be entirely personal to the maker and its meaning only a matter of speculation for others. Although masks in the theatre can communicate ideas, represent characters and symbolize the gods and nature, it can never be said that everyone in an audience is receiving the same messages, no matter how specific in meaning are the shapes, colours and features.

Fig. 13. Mask of Purdah.

Fig. 14. Egyptian funerary mask.

Fig. 15. Stucco painting of a young warrior wearing a helmet-like bird mask, wings and talons to show he belongs to a military order that identifies itself with the eagle. *Found inside a building (Structure A) at the hilltop acropolis of Cacaxtla in Central Mexico. Mayan, A.D. 700–900.*

This does not, however, detract from the value or power of the masks and the art of make-believe. The various messages a mask sends out can add to the excitement of the performance. The art of make-believe reflects a primary human need to explore, through pretence, the world of the subconscious and the world around us. This manifests itself both in the ritual sense, where changes of state are believed to be real and one actually *becomes* the other, and in the theatrical sense of *acting* or *pretending* to be another.[7] Make-believe is the essential element of all ritual, theatre, festival and comedy.

In ritual, the wearing of the mask allows the priest to become the physical representation of the god each time the mask is worn. Some of the earliest evidence of the use of masks in this ritual sense is found in Central Mexico. Buildings at Cacaxtla, a hilltop acropolis, have paintings dating back to A.D. 700–900, one of which shows a Mayan man wearing a bird suit and bird mask. This is significant because the human figure can actually be seen inside the disguise *(fig. 15)*.[8] Cave paintings, such as those at Les Trois Frères in France, show man-animal figures, but are more ambiguous in that the man is not seen to be actually hidden inside the animal skin.

Many ritual masks survive from Pre-Hispanic Mexico. One example is the beautiful turquoise mosaic and shell mask, said to represent the Aztec Sun God, Tonatiuh or Quetzalcoatl *(fig. 16)*. It is generally believed that this mask was worn by the priest during ceremonies of the god himself.[9] The ancient Egyptians represented the god Anubis, the controller of the mysteries,[10] by jackal-headed masks fashioned from terracotta with slits for eyes. However, these could have been models for masks of linen or cartonnage that would have been much lighter to wear over the head.[11]

Today, for many people in parts of Africa, Central and South America and Asia, masks are still regarded as sacred objects, which embody gods or spirits. Often they form the central focus for shamanism, healing ceremonies, tribal and social cults.[12] The famous dance dramas of the Dogon people in Mali, West Africa, are performed

Fig. 16. Funerary mask of turquoise mosaic, representing either Quetzalcoatl, the Plumed Serpent, or Tonatiuh, the Sun God, or Tlaltecuhtli, the Earth Monster. *Mixtec/Aztec, British Museum. A.D. 1200–1519.*

Fig. 17 *(left).* 'Hare' and **Fig. 18** *(right).* 'Rabbit'. Djon masks of carved and painted wood. *Dogon, Mali, Africa. Private collection. 20th century.*

for the benefit of the ancestors and in celebration of the living and the community as a whole. The dancers wear masks and costumes which transform them into some feature of the living world, such as a person, a house, tree or animal *(figs. 17–18)*. Masked ritual can still be found in the context of modern society. In Sri Lanka masks are employed to fight ailments believed to have been caused by demons *(fig. 161)*.[13] In present-day Mexico they are used in a Christian context as a means of coming to terms with the deep human emotions which surround our experience of death.

As ideas about the relation of humankind to the gods evolve, masks tend to lose their sacred and cult significances. The move then is towards dramatic performances often accompanying ritual and ceremony as a means of keeping alive ancient traditions and teaching their message to the general, perhaps illiterate population.

Ritual and theatre are combined throughout Asia, Bali, Tibet and Sri Lanka, where masks are worn to represent the gods in dram-atic performances enacting Hindu epic poems such as the *Ramayana*. Such performances persist even in countries such as Thailand which has been Buddhist for centuries or Java where the predominant relig-ion is Islam.[14] The *Kolam* is a masked dance drama from Sri Lanka where human and superhuman characters, demons, gods and animals are all performed in masks. In Bhutan masks are worn by monks in front of the monasteries in a dance drama on the theme of the struggle between good and evil.[15]

Masks have been made to express ideas not only about the spiritual world but also about the psychological, social, political and economic lives of humankind. The major significance of masks for us in the West, however, is in theatrical performance and largely secular festivals. In modern times, in these contexts, the mask's still potent function is as a dynamic, living art form, used in conjunction with dance, drama, mime, chant, music, poetry and myth.

One of the world's oldest surviving masked theatres is that of the Noh drama of Japan, with its families of masks *(figs. 19–20)*. In its present form Noh is an amalgamation of many different folk and ceremonial mask traditions, going back as far as the seventh century.[16] The masks range in expression from 'neutral' or 'indeterminate' to ones showing extreme animation. Noh masks are slightly smaller than the human face. Carved in wood by skilled craftsmen who pass their skills on down through families, each mask, once made, is carefully inscribed with the signature, date and family of the maker. The Noh actor takes great trouble to select a mask which will enhance his interpretation of the role. Having first put on his costume and wig, the actor sits in front of a mirror and quietly contemplates his role before facing the mask in greeting. All mask acting traditions require specialized skills of body control and concentration, involving in Japan,

Fig. 19 (*left*). 'Young Woman' mask, and **Fig. 20** (*right*). Beshimi male demon mask from the Japanese Noh Theatre. Most Noh masks are carved from Japanese cypress wood and painted with special paints in a specific style known as Nihon-ga. *Japanese Gallery, Kensington, London. 20th century.*

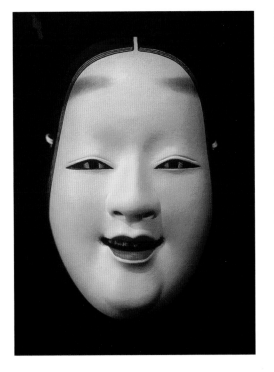

Fig. 21 (*above*). Roman marble statue from A.D. 1–2 showing an actor playing a slave seeking refuge from his owner at an altar. *British Museum, London.*

Fig. 22 (*above*). Marble relief from A.D. 1–2 showing a mask with the typical wide eyes and gaping mouth of later Hellenistic and Roman periods. *British Museum, London.*

for example, a lifetime's training. A performer has to possess strength, agility, perfect timing and control. In visual contrast to Noh masks, other Japanese mask traditions, such as Bugaku, have some grotesque masks of elaborate construction, again carved from wood but with articulated noses, chins, eyes and cheeks, all of which sway and roll with the dance.[17]

Again, the art of the mask is alive in the folk theatre of India which is an example of total theatre, performed outside and combining music, song and prose together with elaborate masks, make-up and costume. It survives because of its popular appeal and capacity to absorb outside influences, such as Muslim or British. It also adapts to modern trends by using microphones and props made from moulded plastic when hand-crafted artefacts are not available.[18]

One of the most captivating traditions of theatrical and ritual masks is to be found in the enactments of mythologies through dance drama by the Native Americans on the Northwest Coast of Canada.[19] Their culture has been on the verge of extinction because of colonization but certain tribes and individuals are rediscovering their heritage and writing down the traditional mythologies, that are rich in symbolism, emotion and humour and are often centred on concerns common to us all. When the tales are acted out, many of the characters appear in masks that embody the meaning of the story in their visual symbolism and imagery. Native American masks are designed to entwine the natural and supernatural worlds; image is placed upon image as a symbol of the interrelation between man and nature. This results in the creation of 'transformation' masks, so-called because they are carved to have moving parts which allow faces to be hidden behind one another, ready for the moment of revelation. Transformation masks epitomize the whole art and mystery of masks. It is the art of illusion where something appears to be what it is not. One image hides behind another, nothing is as it seems and all is illusion, paradox and change.

Masks form part of our European theatrical tradition which stretches from the early Greek and Roman theatre *(fig. 21)*[20] through to the commedia dell´arte of sixteenth century Italy.[21] Greek masks are like sculptures of general or typical character types including gods, tragic heroes and heroines, slaves and satyrs. The actor, almost always male, wore the mask in order to impersonate the stock character which the mask portrayed in the drama. The later Hellenistic and Roman theatre masks were more exaggerated in manner.[22] Only terracotta forms, thought to be used in place of real masks at shrines, survive, and these are to be found in museums. It is thought that the real masks were made from leather, linen or wood but they have not survived *(fig. 22)*.[23]

The Italian masked characters of Punch, Harlequin, the Captain and the rest are humorous archetypes, drawn from nature, formulated in a past age but still recognisable today *(figs. 23–26)*. In fact, the actual commedia characters appear without their masks, time and

time again throughout European dramatic tradition, in the works of playwrights such as Shakespeare, Jonson, Molière and Jarry. Commedia sketches, like much of the comedy in contemporary film and television, satirize attitudes towards money, power, class, race, sex and morality in an ever-changing world.

There is not a long-standing tradition of masked theatre in Britain as it goes against the grain of an acting tradition which has, until now, been based on self-expression and the cultivation of the individual. Peter Brook, who has used masks in his productions, most notably in the *Conference of the Birds*, acknowledges the strain that exists working in a mask tradition that is alien to the art and tradition of Western actors.[24] Nevertheless, in recent years there has been an upsurge of interest in masks, as witnessed by Sir Peter Hall's masked production of *The Oresteia* by Aeschylus *(fig 27)* and *Animal Farm* by Orwell. Innovative masked performances can be seen regularly at the Annual International Theatre Festival in London and some of

Figs. 23–26 *(above)*. Engravings by Callot of Captains from the Italian commedia dell´arte. The Captain is a swagger and a bully and his leather mask has a ludicrously long nose. There are many versions of his type, all of whom make a great show of their courage through boasts rather than deeds. *Jacomo or Jacques Callot, from 'Balli di Sfessania'. 17th century.*

25

Fig. 27. Modern theatre masks of the Old Men of Argos designed by Jocelyn Herbert for *The Oresteia* by Aeschylus, produced by Sir Peter Hall. *National Theatre. 20th century.*

our younger small-scale touring companies such as *Trestle* have pioneered developments in modern masked drama, exploring modern-day archetypes with some considerable success *(fig. 28)*.

Used in the lighter context of festivals, masks are still commonplace in China for New Year celebrations, in West Indian carnivals, Mexican fiestas and Brazilian festivals. These are increasingly crossing international borders and the streets of Britain now play host to Chinese dragons and the Caribbean masks of the Notting Hill Carnival. Many carnivals are associated with specific feast days such as Mardi Gras or Fastnacht. During these times people can wear masks and costumes that liberate them from the constraints of their everyday occupations and responsibilities. An essential element of carnival is the debunking of usually sacrosanct images of religious or secular authority. In Bolivia, for example, mine owners are ridiculed by masks representing the Devil *(fig. 29)*.

Carnival masks reflect in their form and imagery the purpose and social functions for which they are used. The fashionable masks of court society in sixteenth-, seventeenth-, and eighteenth-century France and Italy were elegant and restrained in style. The Venetian *gnaga* or *larva* mask, for example, was rigidly uniform in style and so enabled

Fig. 28 *(left).* Modern helmet-mask or full-head mask made from fibreglass, representing a little girl from Trestle Theatre Company's play *Crèche. 20th century.*

its aristocratic wearer to move freely within the city.[25] Today the masks of the Venetian Carnival are an important economic factor in the tourist industry *(fig. 30).*

Masks of the peasant population and ordinary people tend to be less restrained and more vigorous and characterful in style. The carnivals celebrated today to welcome the spring and other festivals of folklore, often have their roots in pagan feasts and superstition converted over time into Christian ceremony. Feasts to exorcise winter are found, for example, in the Black Forest, Upper Bavaria and the mountain villages of the Tyrol, Switzerland and Slovenia. Here people still make and wear masks renowned for their burlesque characteristics.[26]

The ordered, bourgeois lives of people in other cities in Europe are overturned, for example, at New Year in Basle, Switzerland or Easter week in Binche, Belgium. The inhabitants wear grotesque masks which violate all ideals of beauty.[27] They serve to liberate the wearer from the

Fig. 29 (*facing*). Fully-costumed figure of the Bolivian devil as it would be seen on parade, complete with specially decorated trainers, and mask of painted metal, or cast plastic, and glass. *Rijksmuseum voor Volkenkunde, Leiden, The Netherlands. 20th century.*

Fig. 30 (*left*). Papier-mâché Venetian *gnaga* or *larva* mask, (a white mask shaped to stand out like a beak from the face). The most typical costume in eighteenth century Italy was a large black-hooded cloak called a *domino*, a three-cornered hat, a piece of black lace or silk covering the head and jaw, called a *bauta*, and a white beak-like mask. It became prescribed convention for aristocrats to wear this disguise when they wanted to move more freely within the city. *Venice. Private collection. 20th century.*

inhibitions, laws and niceties of a seemingly well-ordered everyday life but are also a reminder that chaos, destruction and mutability are always with us. Once the festival is over, order is re-established, masks and costumes are put away, and everyone returns to their old lives. In countries where carnivals and folklore have been eclipsed, the need for misrule is still evident but, perhaps, in another guise. The ever-changing culture of young people, alternative images in fashion, music and the Arts reflect the quest for the constant reinterpretation of the age-old masquerade of life itself.

It is fascinating to discover more about the meaning and origins of masks, but in the visual arts, the association of masks with folk culture has to a large extent militated against them being considered as an art form worthy of study in its own right. However, the fact is that many masks are beautiful creations. They are exciting and inventive in texture, colour, shape and materials. As forms in space, masks are a direct stimulus for two and three dimensional exploration. Traditional masks might be carved from wood, then decorated with beads, abalone or cowrie shells, or often inlaid with precious stones and metals. They can be made from paper, leather, plastic and all manner of metals, tin to gold. These and other materials are often indigenous to the environment of the people for whom the mask is made *(figs. 31–35)*.

Modern theatrical masks use an eclectic range of materials from wood or leather to industrial materials such as latex, plastic, fibreglass, resin, cloth, vinyl silicone, foam-rubber and expanded polystyrene. Simple techniques involving paper-construction or papier-mâché are also still employed. These latter are not necessarily

Fig. 31 (*above*). African mask of polished wood or metal. *Gordon Reece Gallery, Knaresborough, North Yorkshire. Date unknown.*

Fig. 33 (*below*). Iroquois mask from Northeastern America, made from coils of braided and twisted corn husks. *Rijksmuseum voor Volkenkunde, Leiden, The Netherlands. 20th century.*

Fig. 32 (*above*). A modern Venetian mask of tooled and painted leather fashioned in the shape of a butterfly. *Private collection. 20th century.*

Fig. 34 (*below*). Sculpture of an actress with tragic mask. *Entrance doorway, Royal Academy of Dramatic Art, Gower Street, London. 20th century.*

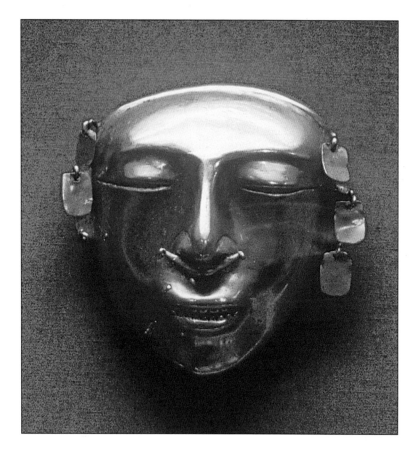

Fig. 35 *(left).* Cast gold mortuary mask with filed teeth, and nose and ear ornaments. *Quimbaya region, Colombia. British Museum. A.D. 500–1500.*

inferior to other methods, nor do they involve any less artistry. Apart from providing a starting point for those wishing to go on to more technically difficult methods, they can in themselves produce very striking results. They are also versatile enough for the mask-maker to make his or her structures look as though they have been created from a different medium, even stone or bronze. Finding ways of creating illusions, of making something appear to be what it is not, is one of the time-honoured arts of the theatrical prop-maker, and the visual wit and ingenuity of such imitation is also a feature of the work of some contemporary artists. Eduardo Paolozzi for instance has made convincing 'granite' heads out of the pulp from paper egg-cartons in exploration of the same idea. Solving the problems posed by the realization of a particular mask-concept can offer many different kinds and levels of pleasure.

Mask-makers in many cultures have traditionally been revered. Often customs, rituals and taboos surround the choosing of the material. In the case of wooden masks the essential drying processes that have to be followed before the wood is ready for carving are rigidly stipulated.[28] Ceremonies accompany the removing of

Fig. 36 *(overleaf).* Masked seal hunter, *Greenland. Rijksmuseum voor Volkenkunde, Leiden, The Netherlands. 20th century.*

Fig. 37 *(overleaf).* An Iroquois false-face mask of red-painted wood and horsehair from Northeastern America. False-face masks are used in connection with rituals to prevent and cure ailments such as nosebleeds, earache and toothache. These masks are believed to hold great powers of protection, command respect and are offered gifts of tobacco. *Made by Jacob Thomas. Volkenkundig Museum 'Gerardus van der Leeuw', Groningen, The Netherlands. 20th century.*

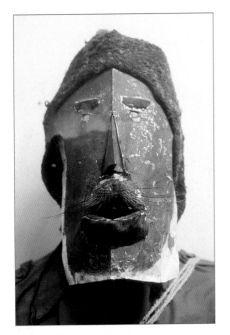

Fig. 36 *(above).* Masked seal hunter.

Fig. 37 *(below).* Iroquois false-face mask.

the wood from the tree for the most sacred masks made in Bali, and the wood is stored in the family kitchen for several months to allow it to be smoked and to dry out properly. All sacred masks must be carved in the temple and subsequently stored there, since the mask is believed always to contain the spirit embodied in the material used or bestowed on it through ritual. Much of the personality of the mask is indicated by its colour: for example, white masks are pure, black masks strong and dominant, red masks brave and hot-headed, purple masks hard and loud.[29]

In these cultures there is also great sympathy between the mask-maker and the actor who will eventually wear the mask. Whilst working, the mask-maker will focus upon the actor and his role, as well as the village for which the mask is made. The actor reciprocates by spending time absorbing the mask's character traits and features. In this way the mask develops its significance. Actors store the masks in boxes when they are not in use, and these must be carefully placed where no-one steps over them. It is believed that only through constant use can a mask retain its power, and masks are not left for long periods in storage or used for decoration. Moreover, before every performance the actors must undergo an elaborate ritual. In Bali, before wearing the mask the performer first sprinkles holy water upon both it and his own face.[30] There are clear distinctions between masks made and used for serious performance and non-sacred masks, which now form part of the tourist trade in the Far East.

It would be a mistake to think that only an artist can make a mask. As a part of folk culture masks are made throughout the world by anyone, often out of whatever materials are at hand *(figs. 36–37)*. True, many cultures hold professional mask-makers in special respect and masks have become a respected art form in themselves, but there is a lively tradition of masks as folk art and no-one should feel that the mystique of the mask-maker's art excludes them. Masks are so much more than objects of fearful taboo or trivial fun. Through the making of a mask the student can create another person or a creature, and once made the mask cries out to be used. Through the performing arts the wearer brings the mask to life, and the mask brings life to the wearer.

Masks as Resources

In the West masks are not central to our artistic expression, yet masks form an essential part of the creative and spiritual lives of many people across the world. Also, surprisingly, even though they have meanings which we cannot fully appreciate, it is not unusual for western artists such as Picasso, Henry Moore, or Eduardo Paolozzi to draw inspiration from masks as well as other ethnographic and tribal artefacts. They often do so for aesthetic reasons; the form, texture, colours and use of materials can have a direct and arresting impact on our senses. The artist also reinterprets the meaning of the object, often disregarding context and purpose. He or she can ignore or reject aspects of a piece which, for the mask-maker, the masked performer and audience, as well as the curator, the archaeologist or the anthropologist, are its most important attributes.[1]

This free use of ethnographic material could be criticized as showing a lack of scholarship and respect for objects that may have sacred meanings for some cultures. We do not take ideas so freely from the sacred images of our own culture without being aware of the element of controversy that might be involved. Also, it has to be said that in some cases, masks and other tribal artefacts have been used for cult practices involving, for example, initiation or circumcision rites, which whilst being highly significant for participants, might be sacred and taboo, and thus difficult to comprehend for anyone outside the group *(fig. 39)*. The more we, as outsiders, know about their meaning, the less easy it might be for us to look on the actual mask or artefact with the same total disregard for its original purpose. The question artists have to ask is whether, if they knew more, it would make any difference to their response *(fig. 38)*. Taboo, superstition and spiritual values are not the same across tribes or cultures, and the artist in all societies is bound to reinterpret what he or she sees.

Similar questions arise for the educationalist. Masks seen in museums are taken out of their living context. Masks are rarely made to be exhibits; they are complete only if seen with the whirl of costume, movement, colour, sound and music of a performance with the people for whom they were made. Our museums are full of ethnographic material taken out of context, which gives us tantalizing glimpses of other worlds, and this can give us an appetite

Fig. 38. Full-face mask with white-painted face. The whole mask, including the top of the head and the hairstyle is carved in wood. These masks are associated with funerary rites. *Ba-Lumbo, Gabon, Africa. Museum voor Volkenkunde, Rotterdam.*

Fig. 39. Helmet mask made from wood, cloth and leather and decorated with beads, small cowrie shells and patterns of triangles and diagonal lines. *Bena Lulua of Kuba, Democratic Republic of the Congo (formerly Zaire). Museum voor Volkenkunde, Rotterdam.*

to find out more. Undoubtedly museums open up other horizons for us all, and museums themselves have increasingly recognised the need to make exhibitions accessible and more informative.[2] Often the information is simply not all there, as many objects were never properly documented. Does the fact that we cannot know the meaning of each object preclude us from referring to it? Does it mean that we are under an obligation to discuss the political and moral issues surrounding collections of ethnographic materials?

When using ethnographic resources there are some basic

considerations of which we should be aware. First of all, no matter how much first-hand knowledge an anthropologist might have of a particular culture, it can never be claimed that he or she has a complete understanding of all the facts. Generally speaking, anthropologists are less interested in establishing 'laws' about the way people live, than interpreting what they observe and searching out meanings.[3]

Moreover, artefacts from other cultures can look very different from the objects we or our students are used to. They have their own language of imagery, symbolism and form to express their meanings. Masks, especially, are highly symbolic and were made to communicate ideas and value systems often remote from our own.

We should be aware that the arts play differing roles in the communal lives of different peoples. For some, the monetary value of an artefact is a prime consideration; for others art has more to do with the way people live, their beliefs, society and institutions. Ironically, artefacts that have little monetary value in their place of origin can fetch high prices in foreign galleries.[4] Care has to be taken, therefore, to ensure that use of ethnographic or unfamiliar artefacts challenges rather than reinforces stereotyping and cultural prejudice.[5]

A willingness to open up these areas can improve our understanding of the diversity of people. We must ask what these objects mean, why, how and for whom they were made, who collected them and for what reason? Masks can continue to excite our imaginations and to suggest an almost infinite range of creative possibilities. Mysteries will always remain, but an awareness of the issues can shock us into the realization of how much has been and continues to be destroyed, alerting us to the fragility of organic human systems.

Carefully presented ethnographic artefacts can teach us to value and wonder at the diversity of human creativity. Masks have been and continue to be made by many people across the world to celebrate, to dramatize and to mourn. This can inspire us and give a positive value to our own work; and it can remind us not to be neglectful or self-conscious about our own individual need for creative expression *(fig. 40)*.

Planning a Project

Mask-making is a 'way in' to the exploration of many different aspects of a subject. For example, if Native Americans are studied, it is possible to explore not only masks, but also their history, geography and culture. If children's books are used as a starting point, then half-masks can lend themselves to character work.

Once the project is decided upon, but before starting mask-making, it is important to consider the following questions:

a) What is the mask going to represent?

Masks can represent the mask-maker's idea of a character, an animal or a creature from another planet. They can depict animals, fish, insects and all manner of natural forms. Rather than aim for verisimilitude, it is more productive to enjoy the process of making and allow ideas to grow. You might begin a project without a specific character in mind, allowing the mask to emerge during the process of making. Once made, you can then 'read' the character in the mask (fig. 40).

b) How is the mask going to be worn?

The manner in which the mask fits the wearer is extremely important. Comfort, lightness coupled with strength, ease of breathing and unobstructed vision are essential in a mask that needs to be worn for any length of time.

Masks do not have to be worn – they can be held in front of the face by means of a stick. Some masks are worn more like hats and do not touch the face at all. It depends on the preference of the wearer.

Using Traditional Mask Models

Traditional mask forms can provide ideas as to the kind of mask best suited to your purposes.

Full-face Masks

Full-face masks cover the face, using the performer's hair, a wig or the costume to complete the effect. These masks are used, for example, in Japanese Noh Theatre. Often the performer has to grip a 'bit' or ledge inside the mask with his teeth. This means that the mask can be held in place in front of the face and allows

Fig. 40 *(facing page)*. Cola can mask made from recycled materials, designed and worn by an undergraduate student. *Workshop led by Andy Earl, Hull School of Architecture, UK. September 1996.*

37

Fig. 41. Painting of a Noh play in performance. *Japanese Gallery, Kensington, London. Date unknown.*

for more variations in head movement. The mask is secured by tapes round the head. The actor cannot speak and so mimes the part. The words are spoken by another performer on stage at the same time. Percussion sounds or instrumental music can form an accompaniment. Using performers on stage in this way can be a challenging drama exercise *(fig. 41)*.

Half-masks

Half-masks cover the face down to the upper lip. They can depict ears, eyes and noses. These are traditionally used in very energetic styles of acting such as the Italian commedia dell'arte. Some half-masks are smaller still and merely surround the eyes. These are often

Fig. 42. 'Aslan the Lion' half-mask from *The Lion, the Witch and the Wardrobe* by C. S. Lewis (music and lyrics by Irita Kutchmy). *Mask designed and made by the author out of cloth glued onto a paper construction base. Costume by Chris Lee. Hull Truck Theatre Company production. January 1987.*

Fig. 43. 'Mr and Mrs Beaver' half-masks from *The Lion, the Witch and the Wardrobe* by C. S. Lewis (music and lyrics by Irita Kutchmy). *Masks designed and made by the author out of cloth glued onto a paper construction base. Costumes by Chris Lee. Hull Truck Theatre Company production. January 1987.*

used in dance as, for example, in the masked ball in *Cinderella* with music by Prokofiev. They are secured by elastic loops round both ears, or elastic round the back of the head and allow the dancer freedom to move and breathe. Both types of half-masks are extremely useful and easy to use in dance or drama *(figs. 42–43)*.

Helmet Masks

Helmet masks cover the entire head. These are used in special effects for film and television, as well as by some contemporary live theatre groups. Huge helmet masks are often seen paraded at carnivals.

Crest-Headdress Masks

Crest-headdress masks do not touch the face at all, being worn like hats on top of the head. Some Native American masks, resembling totem poles with more than one face, are constructed in this way.

These masks pose a stimulating design problem involving tall constructions, supports and scaffolding techniques. All these can be carried out in paper construction. The finished masks can be spectacular and because the face remains uncovered they are easy to use.

Masks for Groups

Some masks are worn by more than one person. The magnificent Chinese Lion Mask is held by two dancers, while others support its long undulating body. A lightweight cane-and-barkcloth 'iguana' mask used in New Guinea covers four dancers, giving the effect of eight legs. These are great fun to make and a lively challenge to try and move underneath as a group *(fig. 44)*.

Stick Masks

Stick masks do not have to touch the face at all. Half- or full-face, they can be attached to sticks and held in front of the face for teasing effect. These masks are ideally suited to dance, ritual and carnival. They are invaluable when used to encourage formal movements and gestures *(fig. 45)*.

Fig. 44. 'Iguana', cane-and-bark cloth mask with a group of dancers. *Papua New Guinea. Staatliche Museen zu Berlin. 1912.*

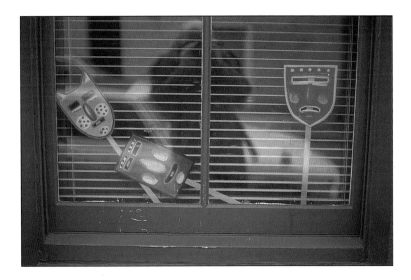

Fig. 45. Stick masks seen in an artist's studio window. *Tufnell Park, London. 1995.*

The Mask and Costume

Traditionally a mask is always seen in combination with a costume so as to present a complete character. The costumes are often made from materials that are ready to hand in the area or culture in which the mask is found. Often feathers, bark, beads and paper are used as well as cloth, skins and raffia *(fig. 46)*.

Other Activities

If the mask is to be used in dance or mime, and particularly if its wearer needs to speak or sing, a half-mask may be more appropriate than a full-mask. If it is to be a large structure, masking more than one person, or to be paraded outside, it needs to be lightweight but well made. Durability may be a prime consideration for masks used in theatrical or carnival events.

Organizing the Working Space

Broadly speaking, space – or the lack of it – is not a limitation to mask-making. Having organized mask-making workshops in village halls, canteens, gymnasia and in the open air at festivals and fêtes, I have narrowed down certain basic requirements:

Tables to work on (or desks that can be pushed together) and chairs;
A large plastic rubbish bag;
A separate table for all your materials.

Preparation

Plan well in advance, as you may have to order some materials. Mask-making should be taken in stages and the projects in the following chapters give a guide to the stages that might be followed.

Fig. 46. Basketry, cloth, beadwork and cowrie-shell elephant mask. A typical elephant mask has two large circular ears and a long flap as a trunk at the front. Maskers wear complete costumes and beaded hats and they sway and gyrate as they dance. *Cameroon. Tropenmuseum, Amsterdam. Date unknown.*

Social skills

The key social skills developed through maskwork are co-operation, clarity in communication of ideas and instructions, as well as trust in a partner. A mask-making session with a whole group of young children can work particularly well if older students or parents are invited into the classroom to help. It can also prove to be a successful way of bringing together special-needs and able-bodied students, or of encouraging a community spirit *(fig. 47)*.

Is the mask successful?

As with any process, mask-making has its ups and downs. Failures become opportunities and ways have to be found to make changes. Students and workshop leaders can develop their own assessment criteria depending on the project. If formal assessment is required then a notebook can be kept. Questions can be put to the group as part of the design and problem-solving process. The most telling assessment is if, in the end, the mask 'works'. Can it be worn comfortably? Can the wearer still see? Hear? Breathe? Then we can ask the audience to evaluate the mask. Does it convey character? Do the movements bring that character to life?

Fig. 47. Children and adults at an open-air paper mask-making workshop, led by the author. *York Early Music Festival. Summer 1987.*

First Steps

Exploring the medium, tools and skills before making a mask
These are lively activities that can act as forerunners to mask-making for everyone. Paper-sculpture techniques are explored in order to promote knowledge and understanding of paper and its properties. For the youngest children this offers opportunities for language development and the kinetic response to simple shapes.

1. Exploring Paper

OBJECTIVES

- 'Ice-breaker' activity for adult groups *(fig. 48)*
- 'Fun' activity for younger groups (e.g. finger dexterity, language development)
- Exploration of the properties of different kinds of paper
- Manipulation by hand
- Encouragement of improvisation and flexible attitudes to working the material
- Language generation

'ICE-BREAKER' *(For adults as individuals or in small groups)*

The only material required is paper – lots of it and as many different kinds as possible. This is a timed activity; the emphasis is on the enjoyment of making as many different 2- and 3-dimensional shapes or objects, using only the hands to manipulate the paper, (e.g. tear, fold, bend, pleat, twist, etc.)

(5 minutes)

- Tear up the paper into long strips.
- How many different methods can be found for joining them, (e.g. weave, plait, interlock, loop, etc.)?

(5 minutes)

- With 'x' amount of paper make:-
  a) 3 flat shapes (e.g. circle, square, etc.).
  b) 4 shapes with space inside (e.g. box, cone, etc.).
  c) 2 shapes which cut through space (e.g. arch, spiral, etc.).

Fig. 48 *(facing page).* Masks of coloured paper, designed and worn by undergraduate students. *'Ice-breaker' workshop led by author. Field trip, Keldy Castle, Yorkshire, Hull School of Architecture. Autumn 1987.*

Fig. 49 (*above*). 'Paper and touch'. *Pupil at Tweendykes Special School, Hull. Spring 1989.*

Figures 50–54 *(facing page).*

Fig. 50 (*top left*). Folding the paper into pleats. *Hilda Anne, Hull. Summer 1986.*

Fig. 51 (*centre left*). Rolling the paper. *Hilda Anne, Hull. Summer 1986.*

Fig. 52 (*bottom left*). Linking the paper. *Hilda Anne, Hull. Summer 1986.*

Fig. 53 (*top right*). Controlled tearing. *Eleanor, Hull. Summer 1986.*

Fig. 54 (*bottom right*). Building with paper. *Eleanor, Hull, Summer 1986.*

(10 minutes)

– Build a tower, bridge, cave, etc.

'FUN' ACTIVITY (*for young people*)

Collections of paper from sample books and rolls of newsprint, tissue, crêpe, cellophane or any other paper of any texture or colour can be used for exploration. No tools are necessary at first; the aim is to explore through the senses, developing finger dexterity, and furthering eye and hand co-ordination.

Always encourage talk about the process itself. With younger children it is vital that the teacher's questions are phrased like challenges, such as: 'How can we . . . ?' 'What happens if . . . ?' 'How many ways . . . ?' The challenge is the medium through which exploration is conducted and by which an element of fun can be introduced!

Exploration Through the Senses

Sight

Look and talk about the different colours found in paper. For example, is the paper as white as chalk or more like milk or cream? Does it shine as white as pearl or is it as black as coal?

Touch

Close eyes and touch the paper. For example, does it feel smooth and slippery or rough and bumpy? Does the paper feel glossy like silk? Is it corrugated and uneven, or is it flat? (*fig. 49*).

Hearing

Listen to the sounds paper makes as it moves. For example, paper can crinkle, flap, flick and rustle. Does it making a fluttering sound or a pitter-patter sound, like rain?

Smell

Talk about the different smells and their associations. For example, paper can smell of trees and forests. Does it smell like wood, oil, ink, paint or fruit?

Developing Finger Dexterity

Controlled tearing requires nimble fingers and a sense of direction! It will be interesting to discover that most paper tears more easily in one direction than another because of the lie of the fibres as they settle during paper-making. When making anything out of paper the irregular torn edge can be more expressive than a straight line.

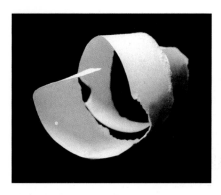

Fig. 55 (*above*). 'Spiral'.

Fig. 56 (*below*). 'Linked form'.

Experimenting with Ways of Tearing Paper

Tear the paper slowly, then quickly, but carefully. Tear in a straight line. Make a zigzag edge, then a curvy edge. Tear a piece of paper to make two pieces. Now tear one to make four pieces. Tear the paper along a diagonal line. Try tearing the paper into a funny shape.

Manipulating Paper into Different Shapes and Forms

Paper will bend, roll, crease, twist and curl. It can be folded into pleats and stood up *(figs. 50–54)*. These shapes and forms can resemble other things; the paper can be jagged like rock crystal, smooth like silk, pointed like a church spire, folded to grow bigger and smaller like a fan, wavy like snowy hills, spiralled like a shell *(figs. 55–56)*.

2. Exploring Skills and Tools with Younger People

Young children need time to familiarize themselves with the safe use of basic tools, such as scissors and pencils. Specific skills should be taught in isolation rather than discovered by chance during the process of making something *(fig. 57)*.

Materials

- ☐ Paper for drawing on and cutting up
- ☐ Paper masking-tape

Tools

- ☐ Pencils
- ☐ Scissors
- ☐ A small piece of Plasticine* for each child

Skills

- ☐ Safe handling of tools
- ☐ Holding and using a pencil and scissors
- ☐ Cutting along lines, in specific directions and cutting out from the middle
- ☐ Using masking-tape

When beginning this project with the very young, it can be fun if, as you introduce the tools, you pretend that you have never seen such curious objects before. For example, if you were introducing how to use paper masking-tape, you could ask questions such as:

Is it sticky?

Can I tear it with my fingers? *(fig. 58)*.

Will it remove easily?

Will it take paint or colour from felt-tipped pens?

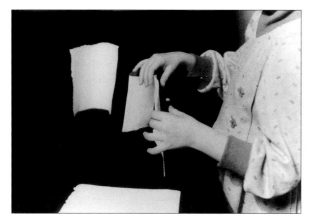

Or with pencils:

What can a pencil do?

Why is it so sharp?

Which way up do I hold it?

Or with scissors:

What are they used for?

How do I hold them?

How do I hold them if I give them to someone?

Fig. 57 (*left*). Making the paper stand up. *Eleanor, Hull. Summer 1986.*
Fig. 58 (*right*). Joining the paper with masking-tape. *Pupil at Tweendykes Special School, Hull. Spring 1989.*

3. Exploring Ways Materials and Tools Work Together

Fig. 59. Cutting out. *Hilda Anne, Hull. Summer 1986.*

Each process involves problem-solving. For example, drawing a line across the paper and cutting along it involves problems such as:

Where do I begin cutting from *(fig. 59)?*

How do I hold the paper?

Which direction or 'pathway' do I follow when cutting?

Drawing a shape in the centre of the paper and cutting it out involves the question:

Which is the safest way to start cutting out from the middle?

(Suggest putting a piece of Plasticine behind the scissor point so that when a hole is made through the paper, the scissor point enters the Plasticine and not a finger!)

Paper Connections

Exploring ways to link or join paper without using tape or glue involves problems such as:

How do I plait or interweave strips of paper?

How do I interlock paper by means of small tears?

Fig. 60. 'Hat'. *Pupil at Tweendykes Special School, Hull. Spring 1989.*

Paper Shapes

It can prove an exhilarating challenge to develop the paper into two- and three-dimensional shapes, although for the purposes of this project we are not aiming to make mathematically accurate models. The following shapes can be made:

> **Flat 2-Dimensional shapes**, e.g., circle, triangle, square, oval, rectangle, diamond, helix, pentagon, hexagon, etc.
> **3-Dimensional shapes containing space**, e.g. sphere, tetrahedron, cube, ellipsoid, octahedron, pyramid, egg, box, cone, cylinder, etc.
> **2-D and 3-D shapes forming space**, e.g. arch, bulge, column, corkscrew, crescent, curl, hollow, spike, spiral, steps, tube, warp, wave, zigzag, etc.

Paper Constructions

Building with paper leads to experimentation with problems of structure, strength and balance, such as:

> How do I make a flat piece of paper stand up?
> How do I fold the paper to make it stronger?
> How do I balance one piece of paper on top of another?

Big Constructions

With small groups of younger children it can be very profitable to explore building small- or large-scale structures from paper, enclosing and opening spaces up and relating structures to each other. Sheets of card or boxes are necessary for this. One way is to build a structure first and then have fun finding out how many different things it resembles:

> Is it a bridge, tower, tent, den or tunnel, a snake, crocodile or dinosaur? *(fig. 60).*

Shape-masks

Improvising with paper mask-making

This form of mask-making stimulates the imagination through the creation of another identity, encourages co-operative work with a partner, promotes manipulation skills and develops eye and hand co-ordination. As the mask takes shape, the difference between a two- and three-dimensional structure is explored. When finished, the mask provides a stimulus for response, in the form of poetry, movement, dance, drama and music. Most of the illustrations show young children. However, making a shape-mask is a universal activity if pitched at the right level. The masks should be made quickly and spontaneously for spectacular results.

OBJECTIVES

- Creating an identity *(fig. 61)*
- Appreciating the relationship between forms in space
- Naming forms and structures
- Exploring materials and tools
- Drawing 2-dimensional shapes and constructing 3-dimensional structures

Emphasis should be laid on the vital skill of improvisation and the enjoyment of the process itself, so groups need not spend time planning or sketching. Shape-masks develop their own identity unique to each person.

Each person will require:

- ☐ Two A4* sheets of thin white card
- ☐ Some different kinds of paper, for example crêpe, tissue, patterned
- ☐ Paper masking-tape
- ☐ Poster paints
- ☐ String
- ☐ Pencils
- ☐ Felt-tipped pens
- ☐ Scissors
- ☐ Piece of Plasticine*
- ☐ Access to a mirror (if available)
- ☐ P.V.A.*

Fig. 61. Large oval-face mask decorated with lines, curves and circles, made from wood, shells, animal tusks and cowrie shells from Oceania. *Cambridge University Museum of Archaeology and Anthropology.*

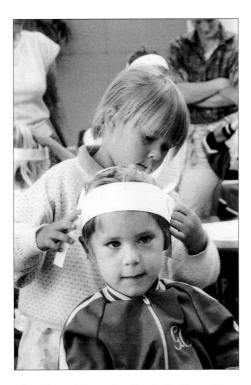

Fig. 62. Making a headband. *Pupils at Grange First School, Grimsby, North Lincolnshire. 1989.*

Making the Mask

Bring the whole group together and with the help of a partner demonstrate how to make a mask following the simple approach outlined here. Take the process one step at a time. Younger groups will need to practice putting out and collecting in materials at the beginning and end of each session; this is an essential part of the learning process and will have to be taught, so allow time for this. Each step should be presented as a problem to be solved and individuals encouraged to find their own solutions.

i) Make a headband

Take one A4* sheet of card. Partners can make a headband for each other from a strip of card about 2.5cm wide. They will have to join two pieces together with the masking-tape to make one piece long enough to go round their partner's head. A headband can consist of a strip of card going round the head and another strip over the top of the head (*fig. 62*).

Use the string to find out the circumference of the head. Use the masking-tape to join the card (*fig. 63*).

Names should be written on the headbands so that they can be given out to the right person in the next session.

ii) Draw the face shape

Use the second sheet of card.

Begin by talking about the different kinds of shape-masks that could be made, for example, round and slimy, with popping eyes and spiralling fur or sharp-faced, long-nosed creatures with triangular ears and jagged teeth.

Decide on the shape. Is the face a geometric shape or a

>

Fig. 63. Joining with masking-tape. *Pupils at Grange First School, Grimsby, North Lincolnshire. 1989.*

Fig. 64 (*left*). Controlled tearing. *Pupils at Grange First School, Grimsby, North Lincolnshire. 1989.*

Fig. 65 (*above*). Positioning the eyes, nose and mouth. *Pupils at Grange First School, Grimsby, North Lincolnshire. 1989.*

shape taken from nature, for example, a cloud, a star, or quite simply a blob?

Young children should be encouraged to make the face shape large enough to fill the card by first experimenting drawing large shapes in the air.

Draw the large 2-dimensional face shape onto the card.

Hold the card and follow the drawn line in order to cut or tear out the shape (torn shapes can be very expressive) *(fig. 64)*.

iii) Position the features

First observe the position of the features on a real face. Partners can mark the position of the eyes, nose and mouth for each other *(fig. 65)*.

Decide on the shape of the features; draw these round the marks and cut them out.

Are the cut-out shapes, for example, the eyes, nose and mouth, large enough to see and breathe through?

iv) Construct the features

Fashion all the features by tearing, twisting and rolling the rest of the card and additional paper. Use masking-tape to hold the paper in shape and fix it to the face.

Nose – A three-dimensional structure? *(fig. 66)*.

Eyes – Large and smiling, small and piercing, cone or spiral; are they large enough to see out of?

Mouth – Smiling or downcast, happy or aggressive, bowed or arched?

Teeth – Large and irregular, small and sharp or curved like fangs?

Ears – Pointed or floppy, small or wide? Devise a way to

>

Fig. 66 (*below*). Constructing a nose. *Pupils at Grange First School, Grimsby, North Lincolnshire. 1989.*

Figs. 69-74. Mask-making sequence.

Cut out the face shape . . .

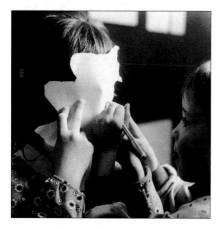

position the eyes, nose and mouth . . .

cut out the eyeholes . . .

cut out two ears which are the same size and shape. Experiment with ways to make the ears concave or convex.

Additions – Horns, antennae, feathers, a crown or a hat? Use more card to construct whatever is wanted, even paper shoulders, arms, wings, or whole costumes! (fig. 67).

v) *Join the mask to the headband*

Once the headband and mask are fixed together, ensure that the wearer can still see and breathe easily.

Compile a checklist to test how comfortably each mask fits. These masks are only meant to be worn for a short time, but they must be comfortable: can the wearer see, breathe and hear? Alter the mask and enlarge the eyeholes, nose and mouth as desired. Partners can help each other to try out their masks.

vi) *Painting and finishing*

Talk about the masks before finishing. What expressions do they have? What creatures do they represent? What shapes can be seen?

How can the mask be painted or coloured so as to bring out its expression?

⟩

Fig. 67 *(left)*. 'Square and Scary Monster'. *Hilda Anne, Hull. 1986.*

54

are the holes big enough to see through?

eyelids and nose can be stuck on with masking-tape . . .

Fig. 68 *(above).* 'A wicked witch casting her spells'. *Eleanor, Hull, 1986.*

Colour can symbolize the character of the mask, whether human or animal. Use the primary colours together with black and white. Cloth, coloured papers and patterned papers can all be added and the mask finished in any way. Too much paint makes the masks lose their shape; younger groups might use coloured paper, cloth or felt-tips to colour their masks. Once dry the masks can be painted with P.V.A. to give them a durable finish *(figs. 69–74).*

the mask is ready for additional features.

ARTS ACTIVITIES

All the following activities are designed particularly for young children. As an extension to art and design, shape-masks can provide opportunities for exploration in movement, dance and drama.

Getting Started

The following forms the basis of a warm-up for a drama session, especially if a group is young. First try out these ideas without wearing the masks. Work in a large, clear space and gather the youngsters together, making them sit in one place. Focus their attention on the size and shape of the space they occupy. Questions might be asked such as:

Is the ceiling high up or low down?

How much space is there between each person?

What shape is the room itself?

What shapes are the objects that can be seen in the room?

The 'Home' Spot

Move the children away from each other to find their own place in the room and ensure that they are not likely to touch or bang into each other. Where they are standing is 'home', and they might be called on to 'return home' at any time. First of all encourage exploration of their own space. Each child should explore the 'bubble' around themselves, without moving from their 'home' spot.

How high can they reach above, below and behind?

How far can they reach to the sides and in front?

Gestures

Gestures start from the body and reach out into space.

Try curling the arms up tightly towards the body, then stretching them away. Try this with hands.

Encourage the same gestures but at different speeds, for example, curl the arms up very slowly and then let them fly out quickly.

Exploring General Space

General space is all the space around us as far as we can see. Before the group is encouraged to move and explore general space it is essential to establish a signal of control which youngsters can learn means they are to stop, or 'freeze' on the spot. You might use a hand clap, a sign, or a percussion sound for the signal.

Try walking away from 'home' and stopping or 'freezing' on the signal.

Try walking or running without bumping into each other.

Pathways

General space can be explored by means of travelling along different pathways in a controlled manner.

Walk along a curving or straight pathway.

Make pathways to form a spiral or a zigzag.

Make a pathway to form a circle, a square or a triangle.

Travel at Different Speeds

Follow a curving pathway very slowly as if moving under water.

Follow a zigzag pathway very quickly as if you are a robot.

Start a spiralling pathway slowly and gradually speed up.

Travel at Different Levels

Follow a spiky pathway, moving quickly and jumping as high as possible.

Make a curving pathway on all fours, as if moving through treacle.

How to Wear the Masks

First check that everyone's mask will fit and that they can see and breathe easily. Masks can be altered as necessary.

Talk about the Masks

At this point the shape-masks turn into 'creatures' and animals. Invent a name for the creature based on the shapes found in the mask. Describe the expression on the creature's face. Describe the creature's personality. Describe the kind of place it likes to live in. What does it like to eat best of all? Has it a favourite pastime?

Bring the Creature to Life!

Wearing the masks, a starting point for a simple movement sequence might be:

Each person finds their 'home' spot in the room and imagines they are a creature, asleep in a den. Where do they live; in a cave, in a tree, under the sea?

The creature starts to wake up and move. What shapes does it make in the air as it moves?

The creature searches for food. How might it move, what kind of pathways does it use, how fast does it travel and at what height from the ground?

At the end of its exploration and adventures the creature returns to its den.

Ideas for Music and Drama

Using sounds or music to accompany the movement, groups can devise an adventure story. For example, one group could be the creatures and the others hunters, without masks.

Figs. 75–76 *(right and facing page).* Shape-masks. *Made by pupils at Grange First School, Grimsby, North Lincolnshire. 1989.*

Some are creatures, the others are traders in exotic animals. The creatures are trapped and transported away for sale. How are they caught? In nets, with guns, traps or drugs? Use mime, movement and sound to show the capture of the creature. Remind students that it is more effective not to touch each other physically when showing this.

Language Development

How many shapes can a creature be? Tall, thin, elongated, broad, fat, curled, twisted or jagged.

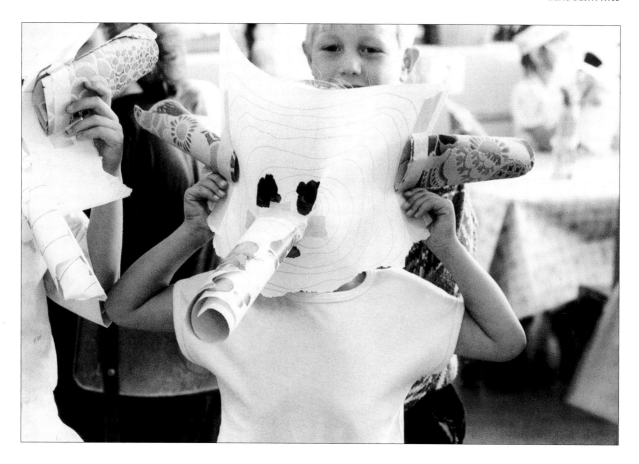

How many ways can a creature move? Fat, slow, like jelly? Sometimes it might not move at all but be as still as stone.

Staying at 'home' the creature can shrink, rise, fall, stretch forward
or backward, circle, twist or spread.

Moving from the spot it can step, skip, jump, leap, turn, twist or
spin.

How many different patterns can a creature make on the floor
and in the air? Straight, angular, zigzag, diagonal, spiky, twisted,
curved or spiral?

Creative Writing

Make up a creature poem:
    What is the creature called?
    Where does the creature live?
    Describe how the creature moves.
    What is its favourite food?

I'm a curvy, curly snail named Spiro!
I live inside a spirally shell.
I slip and slither along and I love
    to eat long, wet spaghetti loops!

I'm a pointed, bright-eyed vulture
My name is Sharp-Claws!
I hang about in thorn trees and
    I'd like to eat you!

Changing Faces

Making a plate mask

The plate mask offers a stimulating focus in drama and creative arts activities for people from eleven years upwards. At a basic level it promotes awareness of body language, and at a higher level, it fosters greater skills of co-ordination, action and response. It is a useful ice-breaker in acting workshops and can act as a quick way into improvisation, mime and a whole range of physical theatre techniques.

OBJECTIVES

- Building a simple plate mask to express emotion
- Exploring the ideas of caricature and stereotypes

The aim is to build a simple plate mask that will express particular emotions through the stylization of features, rather like a cartoon.

Our faces can often reflect our inner feelings. When we experience emotions the muscles in our face move and our features alter. Although we sometimes say that we can read someone's face 'like a book', it is doubtful whether this is ever actually true. Research does not suggest that there is a simple, direct relationship between appearance and emotion. In mask-making we are, therefore, less concerned with real emotion than with caricature and stereotype. This is the first stage in understanding the expressive power of the character mask *(fig. 77)*.

Each person will require:

- ☐ One large flat paper plate
- ☐ Sketching paper
- ☐ A piece of Plasticine
- ☐ Elastic or string
- ☐ Individual hand mirrors (if possible)
- ☐ Felt-tipped pens
- ☐ Scissors

Figs. 77, 82–84. Plate masks used in improvised drama. *Made and performed by students at Newland School for Girls, Hull. January 1991.*
Fig. 77 *(facing page).* 'Family portrait'.
Fig. 78 'Pulling faces' *(above right).* 'Angry'. **Fig. 79** *(right).* 'Happy'.

Fig. 80 *(above)*. Mark the features.

Fig. 81 *(below)*. Boldly draw the features and cut them out.

Making the Mask

Begin by discussing how we convey our emotions; anger, boredom, delight, sorrow, pain, fear, happiness or elation. Use the discussion to generate language describing emotions, for example:

Find other words to describe happy, for example: joyful, delighted, blissful, starry-eyed, ecstatic, pleased, smug, smiling, laughing or hysterical.

Find other words to describe sad, for example: glum, dejected, gloomy, long-faced, miserable, moping or listless.

Describe afraid, for example: frightened, scared, alarmed, horror-struck, with hair on end or terrified.

Describe proud, for example: conceited, arrogant, haughty, stuck up, puffed-up, fat-headed, high-hatted, pompous, swanky.

In what other ways can words be used to describe emotions? We can use phrases such as: 'as happy as a pig in muck', 'as pleased as Punch', 'green with envy'.

Follow this with a demonstration of how to make a plate mask. Use someone from the group as a partner and introduce each step of the process in the form of questions rather than instructions.

i) Pulling faces

People enjoy looking in a mirror and pulling faces at themselves in order to observe what happens to their features when they convey simple emotions. If mirrors are not available then let partners take it in turns to pull faces at each other. The features can alter dramatically depending on the mood: happy, sad or horrified. Using the drawing paper let each partner make a quick, cartoon-like sketch of their partner's face before it loses the expression *(figs. 78–79)*.

ii) Draw the features on the mask

To ensure that the features on the mask are positioned correctly, each person could hold the paper plate in front of their face while partners mark with a cross in felt-tipped pen the places where the wearer's eyes, nose and mouth are positioned underneath *(fig. 80)*.

Next decide on the expression of the plate mask (this could be the same as the cartoon drawing). Draw the features round the marks.

iii) Where to cut the features

Cut out the eyes, mouth and nostrils so that the wearer can see and breathe. Often it is possible to cut slits underneath the drawn eyes or mouth and only cut out the nostrils instead of the whole nose. It is important to

›

emphasize the eyes. Cut a slit underneath the drawn eyes, large enough for the wearer to see out of *(fig. 81)*.

iv) Position the elastic

Make some holes through which to fit the elastic onto the mask. This can be at either side of the mask, on a level with the ears. Elastic can be looped behind the ears or tied to go round the head.

Individuals can make as many of these plate masks as they wish. They should convey a bold expression of the chosen emotion.

●

ARTS ACTIVITIES

Drama

Plate masks can be used to encourage simple role-playing activities. Here are some suggestions for group improvisations:

Building a Character (Partners)

Each partner takes a good look at the other wearing a mask and thinks up an appropriate name, for example, Happy Errol, Smiling Sue, Joe Misery or Ricky Terror. Partners help each other to devise a manner of walking and moving which suits each other's mask.

'Television Interview' (Partners)

One partner wears the plate mask (ensure that they can breathe and talk!) and the other one is a television interviewer. Make up a scene where the person in the mask is being interviewed. The interviewer makes a list of the questions which are to be asked. This could include details of their personal life, as well as their ambitions and hopes for the future. The scene is then run like a television programme.

Mime

'Surprise Encounter' (Partners)

Work with a partner, one wearing the plate mask. Act out a scene where the two characters meet in the park, but the one in the mask is too happy, too miserable or too terrified about something to speak, depending on the expression of their mask. The unmasked partner has to find out from the other's mime what is responsible for their behaviour. Perhaps he or she has had some bad news or has lost something of value.

Fig. 82. 'Two Friends'.

'The New Friend' (Partners and a family group)

One person takes a new friend (their masked partner) home to meet the family. First of all establish a number of things about the new friend:

> Where do they come from? Outer space, another planet?
>
> What do they like to eat? Ordinary food or only ice cream or paper?
>
> Do they speak? If so, is it in a language which everyone can understand?
>
> Improvise a scene to show how the family responds to their unusual guest *(fig. 83)*.

Fig. 83. 'Introducing a new Friend'.

'Odd One Out'

An intriguing variation on the idea of 'The New Friend' is to play the same scene but have everyone wearing a mask except the 'friend' and so make the masked family the 'norm'. The family will have to devise their own way of communicating, and the one without the mask becomes the odd one out *(fig. 84)*.

On a more serious level this improvisation might be used to introduce a discussion of the ways that people are perceived as being different from each other. This can lead to racism or typecasting people because of how they look or what they wear.

Fig. 84. 'The Odd One Out'.

Creative Writing

When the drama exercises are finished, students might be able to write about the situation they were in and their feelings at being the odd one out. The following are examples of how they could describe the emotions shown in the masks in the form of poetry:

Happiness is:	*Fear is:*	*Pride is:*
Smiling eyes,	*Shadows on curtains.*	*Nose in the air,*
A turned-up nose.	*Mouth saying 'O'.*	*Chin to the sky,*
Mouth like a bow.	*Dark corridors.*	*Looking down your*
Wrinkles!	*Hunger and loneliness.*	*nose at others.*
	Staring eyes.	

Symmetry & Collage

Paper-construction and magazine collage mask-making
Making a simple symmetrical half-mask from card is an easy 'way-in' to mask-making for anyone. (Also, it can be an enjoyable first step in a young child's understanding of the mathematical concept.) Collage masks, however, can be asymmetrical and offer greater possibilities for expression. Suggestions are offered for activities which use masks in conjunction with music, drama, dance and mime.

1. Making a Symmetrical Half-mask from Card

OBJECTIVES

- Introducing the concept of symmetry using a simple method
- Making a cat or butterfly mask *(fig. 85)*
- Using the symmetrical half-mask in dance and drama

In the first part of this project the objective is to explore the creation of very simple symmetrical half-masks which can be worn for dance and drama projects, as well as at festivals and carnival events. (In 'Project 6: Mask and Character', a half-mask is made using the moulded paper gum-strip method which lends itself to more sophisticated animal and character masks.)

Are the two sides of the face identical? Cover one side of the face, then the other, with a hand or large piece of paper and compare the differences between them. It might be found that, for example, the eyes are a different shape. In this project we aim to introduce the concepts of symmetry and asymmetry through mask-making. Whilst our faces might not be symmetrical, we can make symmetrical masks where the two sides are identical.

Each person will require:

☐ Rough paper for experimentation
☐ An A4 sheet of thin card
☐ Elastic and felt pieces
☐ Masking-tape (Manageable lengths of masking tape can be attached to the edge of the table or desk. Use enough to get groups started and don't hand out complete rolls!)
☐ Felt-tipped pens and/or poster paints

Fig. 85 *(facing page).* 'Butterfly': symmetrical half-mask made from paper, pipe-cleaners and sequins. *Open-air mask-making workshop, York Early Music Festival. Summer 1987.*

☐ Scissors
☐ Pencils
☐ Other items for decoration as required, for example, feathers, sequins and fabric fur.

Diagram 1.

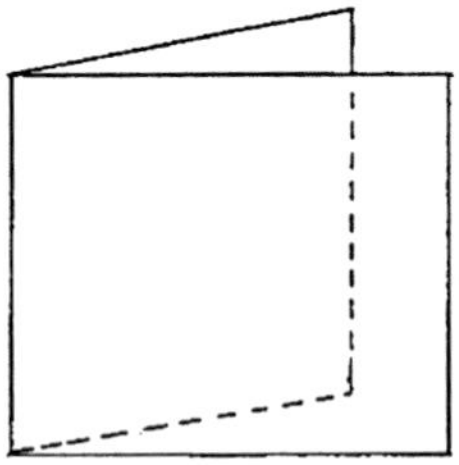

Diagram 2.

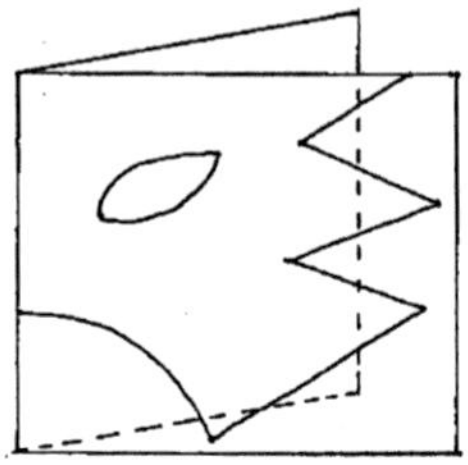

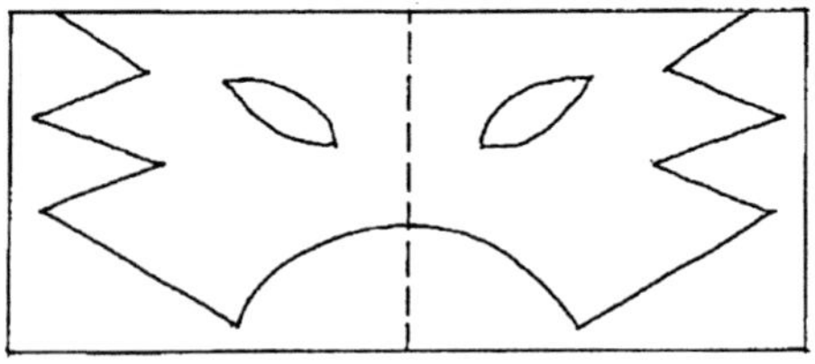

Diagram 3.

Making the Mask

Allow groups to experiment by folding the scrap paper and drawing their half-mask shape onto it before using the card. In this way they can address such problems as:

How do I fold the paper?
Where do I begin drawing?
Where do I position the space for the nose ?

i) How to make a symmetrical half-mask

A half-mask can include the nose and upper lip, or it can be smaller, surrounding only the eyes.

Fold the card in half (Diagram 1) and draw the side view of the face down to the upper lip. Include a space for the nose and draw an eye shape, as shown (Diagram 2). Whatever shape is chosen, as long as the principle of first folding the card is adhered to, the resulting mask will be symmetrical. Cat or butterfly masks with bold symmetrical patterning are effective. Birds, rats and mice can also be fun to make.

ii) Cut out the face shape

Keep the mask folded and cut out the mask shape by means of controlled tearing if necessary. Remind younger participants not to cut the folded edge!

iii) Draw the eyes and cut them out

The eyes must not be positioned too near the folded edge nor too near the cut edge of the mask.
The mask can now be opened out (Diagram 3).

iv) Construct the features

Even a simple base like this can include a nose, whiskers, ears, eyes, eyebrows, feathers, fur and hair, all of which can be constructed out of extra card or different textured paper. Encourage experimentation in folding, twisting, curling and shaping the card into three-dimensional shapes. Use the masking-tape to join these shapes to the mask base *(fig. 86)*. The challenge is to keep the facial features symmetrical.

⟩

v) Supports for the mask

Is the mask to be worn on the face, or is it to be supported on a stick and held away from the face? If a stick is used as a support, it is necessary to build the stick into the mask before the surface of the mask is finished. If elastic is used it can be made either into loops which fix round the ears or into a band to go round the back of the head.

vi) Test the mask

Wear the mask and devise a checklist:
    Can the wearer see through the eyeholes of the mask?
    Does the mask fit round the wearer's nose comfortably?
    Will the mask stay in place?
    If not, alter the mask as necessary.

vii) Finishing

Symmetrical patterns can be added with felt-tipped pens. The inside of the mask can be lined with felt *(fig. 87)*.

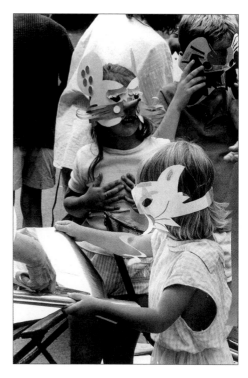

Fig. 86 *(above)*. 'Cat and Mouse': symmetrical half-masks, designed and worn by children. *Open-air mask-making workshop led by the author, York Early Music Festival. Summer 1987.*

Fig. 87 *(left)*. Adding materials to the mask. *Open-air mask-making workshop, York Early Music Festival. Summer 1987.*

ARTS ACTIVITIES

Creative Movement and Dance

Creatures such as butterflies, cats, lions and tigers can be made as simple, symmetrical masks which, in turn, can stimulate groups to explore animal dances and animal movements. Before inventing these dances it is best, if possible, to spend some time observing the animal (on video or in real life) to see how it moves. Observe how it sits, runs, climbs, eats and drinks, then use these observations as movement ideas for devising sequences and stories in dance or mime.

Some possible sources for music and story might be:

Benjamin Britten, *Noye's Fludde*; Andrew Lloyd-Webber, *Cats;* Carl Nielsen, *Masquerade*; Francis Poulenc, *Babar the Elephant;* Phillipe Rameau, *The Hen*; Maurice Ravel, *The Mother Goose Suite*; Camille Saint-Saens, *Carnival of the Animals.*

Poems about animals can be used as a stimulus for ideas:

William Blake, *Tyger! Tyger!* in *The Complete Poems* (Penguin, Harmondsworth, 1998), and in *Selected Poems* (Charles E. Tuttle, Boston, 1991).

Robert Browning, *The Pied Piper of Hamelin* (Random Century, London, 1996, and Alfred A. Knopf, New York, 1993).

T. S. Eliot, *Old Possum's Book of Practical Cats* (Faber & Faber, London, 1998, and Buccaneer Books, Cutchogue, 1992).

Ted Hughes, *Esther's Tom Cat* in *Selected Poems 1957–1981* (Faber & Faber, London, 1982) and *The Oxford Book of Contemporary Verse, 1945-1980,* (Oxford University Press, New York, 1980) and *Hawk Roosting* in *Selected Poems 1957-1981,* and *The Oxford Book of 20th Century English Verse* (Oxford University Press, New York, 1973).

Edward Lear, *The Owl and the Pussy Cat* (Simon & Schuster, London, 1998, and North-South Books, New York, 1995).

George Macbeth, *Collected Poems 1958–1970* (Hutchinson, London, 1998, and Simon & Schuster, New York, 1972), including *Owl* and *Fourteen Ways of Touching the Peter.*

Characters in children's fiction can inspire mask-making:

Lewis Carroll, *Alice in Wonderland* (Random Century, London, 1998, and Random House, New York, 1995).

Roald Dahl, *James and the Giant Peach* (Puffin Books, Harmondsworth, New York, 1998).

Ted Hughes, *The Iron Man* (Faber & Faber, London, 1995), and *The Iron Giant: A Story in Five Nights* (Harper Collins, 1988).

Rani and Jugnu Singh, *The Amazing Adventures of Hanuman* (BBC Books, London, 1988).

2. Exploring Asymmetry Through Masks Using Collage

OBJECTIVES

- Using magazine collage to create features and faces
- Exploring character and movement

Full-face asymmetrical masks can be made easily and effectively from collages of photographs. Magazines and advertisements are excellent sources for detailed photographs of faces, features and expressions. These masks can be a good introduction to the idea of character *(figs. 88-90)*.

Each person will require:

- ☐ Two A4 sheets of thin card
- ☐ Magazines for cutting up (e.g. those with large photographs of faces)
- ☐ Copydex or other glue
- ☐ Pencil & scissors
- ☐ Elastic or string

Making the Mask

Begin by cutting out all the photographs in the magazines which show large faces or features.

i) Draw the face shape

Draw a large face onto the card. Make sure the face is large enough to fill the card.

ii) Add the features

Stick the cut out features or faces onto the card to make up a collage face. Shape can be given to the face by cutting slits into the edges of the card and drawing together the ends at various points around the face. Left-over bits of card can be manipulated into features and added to the face.

iii) Seeing and breathing

Slits through which the wearer can see and breathe can be cut to run underneath the eyes and nose.

iv) Wearing

Finally put the elastic or string on the mask so that it can be worn.

•

ARTS ACTIVITIES

Drama

When worn, collage masks can look exceptionally expressive and usually stimulate a great deal of verbal response from those observing.

Partner Work

One partner wears the mask and begins to move very slowly, the other describing the variety of expressions which emerge. (This exercise works best if there is a mirror which both partners can look at as they talk.)

Group Work

Divide the class into small groups of four or five. Put two groups together and ask them to sit facing each other. The members of one group wear their masks and improvise a scene while the other group is their audience. It is important, when both sitting and moving, that the group in masks keep their heads and masks facing towards their audience. The audience then observes and comments on the differences of expression which emerge.

Scenes to improvise could be:

> Watching an aeroplane travel across the sky.
> Listening to music that they adore or loathe.
> Saying goodbye to someone leaving on a train.
> Smelling a rubbish tip.
> Smelling freshly baked bread.
> Tasting mustard, honey or vinegar and passing it around the group.

'The Newspaper'

A page from a newspaper is passed along the masked group. Each one responds to it, for example, some might laugh, others cry, some try to hang onto it, some beg or force the others to give it up.

'The Waiting-Room'

All but one of the masked group are sitting waiting for a train. Each is doing something, for example, knitting, reading, listening to music through a personal stereo or train spotting. In comes the other masked character who succeeds in distracting them all and involving them in a game or conversation. When the train arrives they all miss it. Show how differently they each respond to this turn of events.

'The Cinema'

Improvise a scene where all the masked characters pretend to be an audience watching a film, sitting together, facing the front. Having agreed on the genre of the film and storyline beforehand, they then have to convey these by means of mime to the unmasked group who watch them.

Figs. 88–90 *(facing page).* Magazine collage masks. *Designed and worn by students of New-land School for Girls, Hull. Summer 1996.*

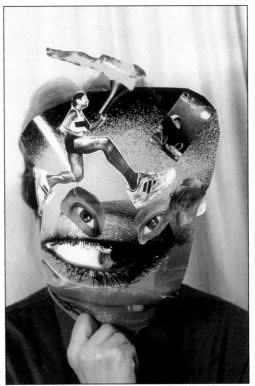

Theatre, Mask & Myth

Constructing helmet masks and crest-headdress masks
This project is most suitable for people from ten-years-old upwards: children, students, and adult theatre groups. Everyone will enjoy designing their own versions of masks from other parts of the world and devising performance-contexts for them by using traditional myths and stories. The making of such masks can be a useful method of promoting understanding of other cultures.

1. Exploring Myths

Myths are concerned with universal themes such as the search for self-knowledge and happiness, or the struggle between good and evil, family conflicts or death. Sometimes, when myths are acted out in places such as South East Asia or North America, the main characters are often masked and their masks embody much of the meaning of the story. Locked into the iconography and the colours and textures of Native American masks, for example, is the spiritual symbolism of Native American mythology. These masks are like poems; the meaning is there to be peeled away, layer-by-layer *(fig. 91)*.

If we are to make use of masks and myths from other cultures such as the Native American, then we must be sure of our reasons for doing so. The museum environment inevitably strips masks of their aesthetic and social context and we can never see them in the living setting of the religious, social and dramatic events for which they were made.[1] We cannot escape the fact that a combination of missionary activity, racism, imperialism and greed has ensured the virtual annihilation of the Native American environment and way of life. What we see are relics of a culture and should serve to remind us all of how much has been lost and destroyed.[2]

In the face of such knowledge, how can we justify using masks as a cultural and educational resource? It might seem to some a matter of conscience not to do so. Yet on the other hand, to ignore them seems to deny the achievement of the cultures that produced them. Masks can be appreciated as beautiful objects in themselves. Their presence in museums can open up the question of how they got there. Were they the spoils of raids, were they collected by missionaries and soldiers? Were they bought, given, bartered or stolen?

Fig. 91 *(facing page).* A sun god transformation mask carved from wood and made by the Kwakwaka'wakw people of the Northwest Coast of Canada. The rays are triangular pieces of wood hinged with leather to close over the face; at the appropriate moment in the ceremony these rays would be lifted to reveal the sun face underneath. The whole mask is painted in symbolic style. *Museum of Mankind, London. Date unknown.*

Figs. 92 *(above),* **93–94** *(facing top left & right).* 'Nature Spirit' masks. Large paper-construction masks painted with metallic car spray paint, designed and made by students from Headlands School, Bridlington, for their *Sea Legend,* performed complete with masks and body paint. *Dane's Dyke, Flamborough, East Riding of Yorkshire. Summer 1989.*

Fig. 95 *(facing below).* 'Nature Spirit' mask. Large paper-construction decorated with metallic car spray paint. *Designed and worn by student in mask-making workshop led by author. Headlands School, Bridlington, East Riding of Yorkshire. Summer 1989.*

If we decide to involve others in enactments of different ways of life, the question we must first ask ourselves is what is the purpose of that dramatic involvement? Are we simply 'playing at being Indians', or are we facing up to important issues, ideas and themes which touch us all? For example, we can broaden the project to bring in issues such as the implications of the domination of one culture or group by another, the exploitation and destruction of the natural resources of an environment and the undermining of an organic culture. We can draw parallels between what has happened to the Native American environment and culture and what is happening now to the once hidden Indians of the Amazon rainforest. At all times we should ask ourselves if we are raising awareness and facing the challenges of history and own times.

Myths and legends can provide a stimulus for the use of language and the appreciation of literary form. Traditional narratives have always been a starting point for a considerable amount of ancient and modern theatre. Groups might, for example, be asked to reinterpret a story and set it in modern times, or to invent a myth of their own *(figs. 92–95).*

Rather than telling people what to re-enact, it might be appropriate for them to collect stories from members of their own families. People with different cultural origins will have many stories, songs, proverbs and riddles from oral traditions and some of the characters might lend themselves to mask-making. Also, groups tend to inhabit their own imaginary worlds, and these they might be prepared to share with each other, to build a play which uses masked characters.

2. 'Raven'

The stimulus for the next project comes from a Coast Salish Swaihé mask legend. The Coast Salish people are Native Americans of the Northwest Pacific Coast. They live in permanent villages, depending for their livelihood on fish from the sea and cedar from the forest. They are renowned for their expert carving of masks, totem poles and the superb craft skills of both men and women. Much of their traditional way of life has disappeared, but their art still flourishes and there is a revival of mask carving and use.[3]

The story is about a destitute child, who, despite many tribulations, wins the respect of the gods and her tribe and is rewarded by the gift of a mask. The story lends itself to the discussion of parent/child relationships, the ways people earn respect and the domination of one group by another. Masks can be made to interpret your own ideas of the gods and spirits, rather than copying the originals. The central character is unmasked and can be played by a boy or girl. The narrative voice is that of a traditional storyteller and should be played as such. The 'Raven' story, and the descriptions of movements and gestures in it, are based on my re-telling and re-interpretation of Native American myths and gestures. This was presented as an amateur theatre production by a Community Arts group from North and East Hull, now no longer in existence, and was a genuine attempt by the group to relate to another culture which they held in the greatest respect *(fig. 96)*. Elements of a similar story can be found in a brief outline in Lévi-Strauss, *'The Way of The Masks'*.[4]

'Raven'

'Watch and listen' were the words her mother spoke before she died, and the girl quietly took them to her heart. From that moment the child was locked into her own world. She listened and watched, but seldom spoke.

As time went on, her father resented his daughter. She was so remote that he wanted to hit her. Often he did, and even then she was silent.

The girl's curious ways set her apart from other children. At first they were puzzled by her, but soon they were laughing and pointing at her.

Her brother was the only one who cared about her. Together they would whisper long into the night, falling silent only when their father came near.

One evening, enraged by their secret looks, the father tore the boy away and forbade him to see his sister. The boy protested but the man lifted his fist, and the boy fell silent.

The father hid his daughter away. She was almost forgotten, and always alone. In the dead of night her brother came in secret to see her. He could not find any food, but gave her the few scraps he had been hoarding. He promised her he would return with more. The girl was weak with hunger, but as she ate the scraps her stomach tightened and she began to vomit.

Seeing she was sick, her father knew she had disobeyed him. He felt cold with anger and hate. Before daybreak he took her to the edge of the village, and throwing her down her few possessions, left her there, saying that he never wanted to see her again.

Alone, on the forest's edge, she watched and listened. Water dripped from the tall canopy of trees. She decided to walk into the thickest part, where the forest closes behind those reckless enough to go there, and to leave not a footprint, not a thread nor hair behind her. She would die far away from home, and her body would never be found.

She felt cold and sick, but it did not matter. A bank of mist changed to cloud as it rolled high up above the mountains. As she pushed deeper into the tangle of dark, dank forest, she was enchanted by the brilliant, moss green carpet beneath her feet. Silently, the wind crept up behind her and blew a wisp of warmth around her, but as the evening drew in, it turned and chased her with its icy chill. She hurried on, hoping to find somewhere to shelter from its biting teeth, but it mocked her every turn. Suddenly, she slipped on a rotted cedar trunk, the moss gave way, and she staggered down between the gaping roots of an ancient tree. She hung there, dazed and trapped. The moss curled back over her, and she drifted into a restless sleep.

In a sudden flash, two Raven spirit gods in masks and costumes appeared to her. As they danced around her they pointed to the sky and spoke as if from under the ground. They commanded her to drag herself free from the roots of the tree. Slipping, twisting and turning in terror, she struggled with all her might until the roots parted with a snap, and she fell free.

The wind fell still, and the child walked on. It was the river's song which drew her to its bank. There she lay down, totally exhausted with cold and hunger, wanting only to die. As she slept, the two masked Raven gods re-emerged from the darkness, and now their voices bubbled up from beneath the water. They ordered the girl to catch two salmon, and told her she was to cook, but not eat them. Only by doing this would she beat her hunger.

The Sun weaved its way between the tall tangles of bush, and its warm light fell on the child. She slowly woke. Every bone in her body ached. The river sang quietly and the girl knelt down to listen. As she did so, she spotted two salmon hovering as if trapped between the rocks and weed. Remembering her dream the girl did as the masks had instructed.

The salmon twisted and curled over the fire. The smell was delicious but, holding back her hunger, the girl did not touch them. Suddenly, before her eyes, the salmon sprang to life and somersaulted back into the water. As she watched, the child's hunger melted away just as the masked gods had promised.

Slowly, the emerald green moss turned into black velvet as the child continued to make her way deeper into the forest. It was bitter cold, and the frost lay its hand on all that moved. The moon threw a shower of crystals along the edges of the branches and leaves. The girl felt the air stiffen with cold around her as she walked on, never turning and never looking back.

Soon she came to a place where the river seemed to be swallowed up by the rocks as it vanished into the earth. By now the moon had slipped behind a cloak of clouds and mist, and darkness fell. Overwhelmed by sleep the child slipped to the ground, thinking only of the welcome sleep with death.

Voices echoed far beneath her, and the two masked gods rose above her. They ordered her to leap into the river at the point where it smashed into the rocks. She awoke, and without a pause did as the gods had said.

Icy spears of water shot her through with cold and terror. Suddenly and violently she was sucked down by the current and hurled against the rocks. Then, without warning, her breath clawed back into her body, and she found herself rising up to meet the air at the mouth of a dry, underground cavern.

Small stones snapped at her feet and knees as she crawled from the water. A sound like a wind humming through reeds surrounded her, and there before her stood a wise old woman bent with age. As the child stared, she saw that the cave walls were hung with precious furs of the sea otter and brown bear. Scattered on the floor were boxes inlaid with abalone shell and copper. She gazed at the old woman and saw that she was adorned with silver and brass bracelets and neck hangings.

The wise old woman said this was not the time to give the girl anything. Instead, she commanded her to go back home and challenge her father, and face up to him. She must order him to fetch a basket and the best blanket. She was then to take them and go to the stream next to the village, and cast a line into the water.

The girl welled up with anger at having to carry out another task. She screamed at the old woman, but the woman watched and listened, and never spoke. The child became calm and did as she said.

The girl found her way out from the dry cave into the sweet air on a mountainside, and returned to her village. The people stared and pointed, but they dared not speak. When he saw her, her father was so afraid that he shook in his boots, slobbered and whimpered, convinced that she was a ghost. He ran and did all that she told him to do, all the time pleading with her to spare his torment.

The girl took her brother to the stream, carrying the blanket and basket just as the wise old woman had said. When they each cast a fishing-line into the water, the water at once began to boil, the surface broke, and up rose two water people, hooked by their tongues. Writhing in agony, the water people begged to be freed. The two children were stiff with terror, but fearing for their lives, they reached out to unhook the tormented creatures.

Once released, the water people were swallowed up by the swirling current, and sank out of sight. Then, in a breath, they returned, dragging up from the depths a large and fabulous mask which they presented to the children. Then, without a sound, they slithered into the water, to the bottom of another world.

The girl and her brother wrapped the mask in the blanket and put it into the basket. Between them, they carried it back to the village.

Everyone came to stare at the mask. From that moment the girl was treated with respect, and when she spoke the others would always listen. It was discovered that when the mask was in the the hands of the girl, sickness and disease were always cured. Such were the powers of the mask.

Fig. 96 (*facing page*). 'Raven God', and seated child with mask of 'Water Spirit'. Masks made from card, felt and feathers by the cast and the author. *Community Arts performance of 'Raven', Hull. 1986. Private collection.*

BACKGROUND NOTES

When working on the myth and before mask-making, the following notes might be helpful during discussion and rehearsal to build a picture for those taking part. Slides available from museums and photographs from the recommended books would be invaluable as visual aids.

Natural Environment

The Northwest Coast of Canada has an icy, craggy coastline. Beaches lead into dark forests and further inland there are swamps. Thick moss covers fallen trees, caverns and rocks. Massive trees grow here such as cedar, fir and spruce.

Weather

The climate is severe, with ice, snow and fog. Seasons change abruptly and there is often bright light and brilliant colours.

Animals and Fish

Animals and fish include the beaver, wolf, bear, ermine, elk, caribou, crow, eagle, owl, swan, whale, sea otter and dogfish.

Communication

Tribes communicated with each other using gesture language and signalling across space.

Social Organization

The people were grouped into tribes and they followed tribal customs, such as the *Potlatch* ceremony where a rich and important man gave away or destroyed much of his wealth to show how rich he was.

Economy

This was mainly a sea-based economy of fishing supplemented by hunting and trading.

Spiritual World

Each person had his or her own totem, for example, sea, animal, tree, cave. Tribes had shamans and sorcerers who passed on the myths and beliefs in cosmology, as well as dance and ceremony *(fig. 97)*.

Arts

For the Indian tribes artistic creation is perceived as a spiritual act. Activities include storytelling, poetry, music, pottery, basketry, jewellery, sand-painting, as well as costume, headdress-making and face-painting. Design work includes symmetrical and split-designs in patterned fabrics and decorative flat beads. Colours are from natural sources and are primarily red, black, blue, yellow and white. All art and craft work is steeped in symbolism, myth and metaphor.

Rivalry

Great store was set in tribal war, contests and games such as wrestling, archery, running, hunting, throwing and team games.

Political and Social Changes

The coming of the white man, such as Juan Perez in 1774 and Captain Cook in 1777, eventually overturned the entire native way of

Fig. 97. Carved wooden totem pole with main crests of the beaver and the eagle. *Haida from Tanu, Queen Charlotte Islands, British Columbia. Cambridge University Museum of Archaeology and Anthropology. 19th century.*

life. It led to the introduction of overseas trade, slavery, missionary activity and colonialism.

3. Mask-making for 'Raven'

OBJECTIVES

- Creating masks to represent characters in a story
- Designing and constructing large helmet masks
- Designing and constructing totem-like crest-headdress masks
- Discovering the cultural and symbolic meanings of the masks

Showing slides or photographs of actual Native American masks will provide an exciting visual stimulus and provide a starting point for designing the masks. Discuss the shapes, materials and colours used and think of the forms associated with the creatures in the story, for example, beak, feather shapes, fins and scales *(fig. 98)*.

The human characters in the play do not need masks. The masked characters include two ravens, the Sun, salmon, the water people and the mask given as a reward. Draw quick sketches of the design of each mask before beginning to construct one.

Each person will require:

- ☐ An A3* sheet of thin card or cartridge paper
- ☐ A (shared) roll of brown paper gum-strip (for joining and strengthening the card during construction)
- ☐ Latex or P.V.A.* glue, plus a brush or spreader
- ☐ Poster paints or other paints as available
- ☐ Spare pieces of paper for experimentation
- ☐ Felt-tipped pens and/or pencils
- ☐ Scissors
- ☐ Needle and strong thread
- ☐ A damp sponge in a plastic margarine container (for dampening the paper gum-strip; the gum should never be licked).
- ☐ Stapler (stapling is a quick way of joining card, or holding it in place. It is not a secure join, however, and the staples should always be covered by paper gum-strip to strengthen them).
- ☐ Additional items could include: felt pieces, fabric fur, beads, feathers, string, wool, strips of cloth, etc.

EXPERIMENTATION

Before embarking on mask-making, members of a workshop can explore the potential of paper (use up any scraps or irregular sized pieces for this). Try:

Tearing – Sometimes it is easier to tear than to cut the paper; a torn edge can be expressive. Torn edges of paper gum-strip mesh together when layered to create a smooth surface.

Folding – Find out how to make a piece of paper smaller or stronger.

Scoring – Use scissors to score the paper. Find out how a scored edge differs from a folded edge.

Pleating – Pleats can be folded so as to be equal or graded in size. Experiment with making a fan shape.

Curling – Strips of paper can be curled on a pencil or with scissors.

Fringing – The small cuts should be equal in length and width.

Making a circle – Use a compass to draw a circle.

Making a cone – Cut the circle so that it can be turned into a cone.

Making a spiral – Cut the circle to make a spiral.

Making a rectangle – Use a ruler to draw a rectangle.

Making a tube – Turn the rectangle into a tube or cylinder.

Making the Masks

A. HELMET MASKS

There are any number of ways to make a mask and include the headband. I have shown two examples. The first shows how to make the headband separately; the second shows how it is possible to include the headband in the design for the original template. The advantage of the second method is that you do not have to attach the mask to the headband at a later stage.

Example One

i) Make a separate headband

Partners can make a tight-fitting headband for each other using two strips of card about 2.5cm wide, taken from the edge of the large sheet. Measure the circumference of the head and make a headband with a strip of card which goes round the head and another which goes over the top.

>

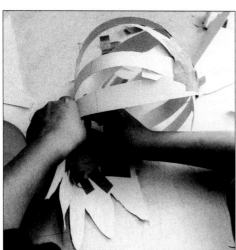

ii) Make the face shape

First, fold the remaining sheet of card in half. Try to imagine and then draw a side view of the face onto the folded card. (When drawing the eyeholes care should be taken not to position them too near the folded edge or too near the cut edge.) Keep the folded edge as the centre line of the face. (Ears, nose, mouth, beak, etc., are all added later) (Diagram 4). Ensure that the face shape is cut out without cutting the folded edge. Remember to cut out the eyeholes safely.

iii) Fix the face shape to the headband

Open out the face shape and attach it to the headband. Make sure that it is positioned to enable the wearer to see out of the eyes. Use card to fill in the back of the head.

⟩

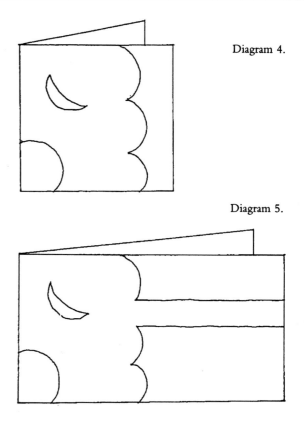

Diagram 4.

Diagram 5.

Figs. 98–101. Four stages in making a 'Water Monster' mask showing a mask with the headband included in the design. *Raven mask-making workshop, Winifred Holtby School, Hull. 1989.*

Example Two

i) Include the headband in the face shape design
(Diagram 5)

Figs. 98–101 show a watermonster mask being made. The headband is incorporated into the design for the face. Whichever method is chosen, once headband and the basic mask form have been made then the features can be added.

ii) Add the features

The card can be folded, cut, scored and manipulated in any way in order to make the mouth, ears, eyes, beak, etc. *(fig. 102)*.

Use the design sketch as an indicator of the shapes to be formed when constructing the features.

iii) Strengthening

As the mask takes shape it will be necessary to strengthen it. Try overlapping small torn pieces of brown paper gum-

⟩

Fig. 102 *(below).* Water monster mask. Mask paper-sculpture base as seen before painting. *'Raven' mask-making workshop, Winifred Holtby School, Hull. 1989.*

Fig. 103. 'Water Monster' mask-like water spout. *Bramham Park, West Riding of Yorkshire. Carved stone. 18th century.*

Fig. 104 (*left*). Painting a completed 'Sun God' mask. *'Raven' mask-making workshop, Winifred Holtby School, Hull. 1989.*

Figs. 105–109. Masks of 'Raven' and other characters. Mask-making workshop led by the author. *Designed and worn by students at Winifred Holtby School. Hull, 1989.*

strip to cover the card as work progresses. This is a very strong and quick way of strengthening the card, but care should be taken not to add more than two layers otherwise the card becomes difficult to alter when dry. Decide the stages at which the mask should be left to dry.

iv) Additions

Add hair and teeth during construction. These can all be fashioned out of card. If any other materials, fabrics or textures are to be used, they should be built into the mask as it is being made. Find out which materials are compatible and so can be glued together. Experiment with sewing rather than gluing materials onto the mask.

v) Ensuring the mask fits

Is the mask still comfortable? Is it becoming too heavy? Is the balance wrong? Is it strong enough?

vi) Finishing the mask

Whatever method of finishing is chosen (for example, paint, felt pieces, fabric pieces, coloured paper, different materials, objects and textures), aim to accentuate the features, especially the eyes. Decide, on the basis of research, which colours and shapes symbolize the creature *(fig. 104)*. A coating of P.V.A. will give the mask a protective varnish, but the mask should be dried out thoroughly before use *(figs. 105–109)*.

B. TOTEM-LIKE CREST-HEADDRESS MASKS

i) Make a separate headband

Use the same method as described in example one to make a tight-fitting headband.

ii) Make the face shapes

Follow the method described in example one for fashioning the face shape of whatever the creature the first totem image represents. Fix this face shape onto the headband so that the bottom edge of the face comes above the wearer's eye level.

iii) Adding the totems

Additional face shapes can be fashioned out of card and fixed above the first one like a totem pole. Folded strips of card can be used to support each face from behind like a prop. The prop can be removed when the mask is strengthened.

>

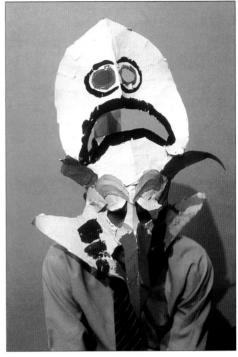

Fig. 105. Totem-like crest-headdress mask.

Fig. 106. 'Child'.

Fig.107. 'Sun'

iv) Strengthening

Strengthen the joints with a layer of brown paper gum-strip (built up in small torn pieces) as the totem grows. More card can be used to construct the back of the heads of the totem faces and strengthened at the same time. (This might be the point to remove the props).

v) Additions

Card can be used to fashion hair, teeth, noses, etc. as necessary.

vi) Ensuring the mask fits

Crest-headdress masks are worn more like hats than masks, which do not cover the face. Strips of cloth, paper or wool can be attached to the bottom edges of the headdress so as to conceal the wearer's face thus allowing him or her to see and breathe.

vii) Finishing the mask

The whole crest-headdress mask will need strengthening with small torn pieces of brown paper gum-strip. Felt pieces, cloth, paint or any manner of textures can be used to finish the headress. Use colours which represent the totem creatures. P.V.A. will provide a clear and protective varnish if needed *(fig. 105)*.

●

Fig. 108. 'Raven with two beavers'.

ARTS ACTIVITIES

Creative Movement and Dance

One way of performing the *Raven* myth would be for one person to tell the story and the rest to improvise it in mime and dance, perhaps with percussion accompaniment. Movement ideas involving gesture language can be very expressive if performed with conviction. The following examples of gestures are based on some of the key words in the story; no attempt has been made to emulate Native American gesture language. In performance the gestures can be used as the basis of dance movements. This list might be useful as a starting point for devising your own system:

I, me – Lay the fingers of the right hand across the chest.

You – Extend the right hand, open and slanted upward.

Mine – Cross the hands on the chest.

Yours – Cross the hands on the chest; then throw them open towards the other person.

Love – Tap the heart several times with a gently clenched right hand.

Hate – Tap the heart twice with the right hand and then shake the head.

Happy – Raise the right hand and make a circular movement.

Weep – Place the hands over the eyes as if sobbing.

No, don't! – Wave the right hand from side to side, then put the hand outwards and in front of the face.

Thank you – Clasp both hands together in front of the chest.

Give me! – Extend the right hand to point towards an object, then bring it back to the chest, fingers pointing towards the body.

Greeting – Bend elbow and hold the left hand up and out from the side of the body.

Go away – Carry the right hand to the left side of the body horizontally, fingers outstretched, then move the hand sharply back to the right.

Sorry – Bow head.

Mercy – Both hands stretched forward with palms upward.

Chop wood – Hold the right hand flat, palm upward, then move it down repeatedly toward the left side in a chopping motion.

Hide – Place the left arm up and cover the head as if to hide it.

Ill – Place the left palm on forehead and the right hand on stomach.

Dying – Close the eyes and put the right hand to lips and move away lightly.

Starving – Put the right hand out in front of body as if pleading.

Eat – Bring the right fist to mouth and make chewing movements.

Bread – Mime holding and breaking a loaf of bread with both hands.

Fish – Hold the right hand up vertically and wave it like a fish tail.

Raven – Lift both arms out to the sides like wings.

Basket – Cup the hands together.

Stream – Trace snake lines on the ground with the fingers.

Home – Bring the back of the left hand up to the right cheek.

FURTHER READING

The following list is a selected bibliography which the reader might find valuable when researching this project:

- Bancroft-Hunt, Norman, and Forman, Werner, *People of the Totem: The Indians of the Pacific North-West* (Orbis, London, 1985, & University of Oklahoma Press, 1988).
- Burland, Cottle, *North American Indian Mythology* (Hamlyn, London, 1965, & Peter Bedrick Books, New York, 1985).
- Dooling, D. M., and Jordan-Smith, Paul (eds.), *I Became Part of It* (Parabola Books, New York, 1990).
- Levi-Strauss, Claude, *The Way of the Masks* (Jonathan Cape, London, 1983, & Washington University Press, 1988).
◊ Liptak, Karen, *North American Indian Sign Language*, (Franklin Watts, New York, 1990).
- Macfarlan, Allan and Paulette, *Handbook of American Indian Games* (Dover, New York, 1985, & London, 1998).
◊ Tomkins, William, *Indian Sign Language* (Dover, New York, 1969, & London 1998).
- Wilson, Eva, *British Museum Pattern Books–North American Indian Designs* (British Museum, London, 1984), & *North American Designs for Artists and Craftspeople* (Dover, New York, 1987).
- Wyatt, V., *Shapes of Their Thoughts* (University of Oklahoma Press, 1984).
- Young, Maxine, *North American Indians–Cut and Colour* (British Museum, London, 1985).

Fig. 109 *(facing page)*. 'Sun God'.

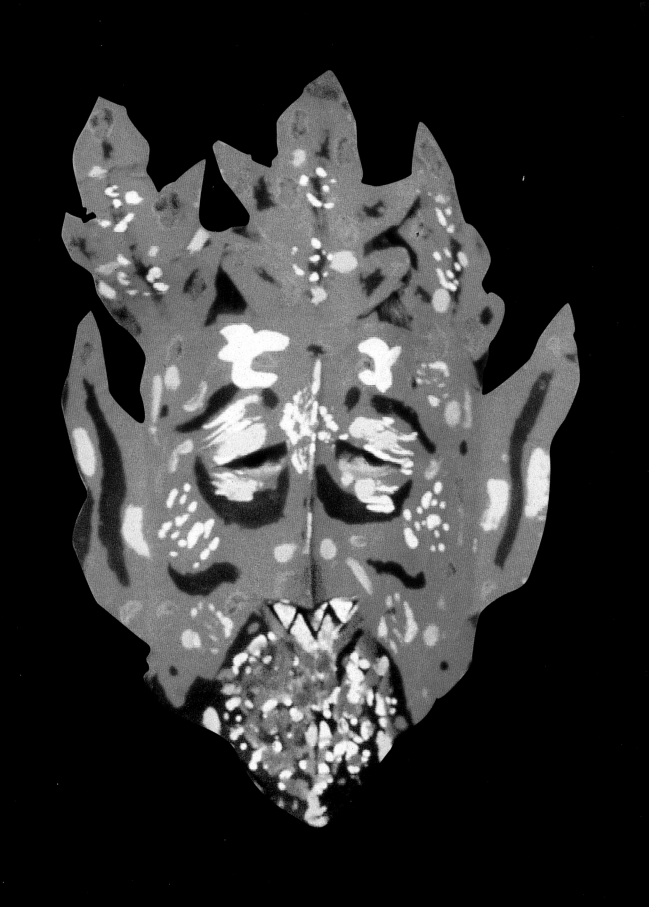

Character & Commedia

Moulded brown paper gum-strip mask-making

This project is most suitable for people aged fifteen years upwards: students, drama groups and actors. The designing of character masks encourages an interest in basic psychology and provides a focus for interrogating social stereotypes. The relevant techniques, if well-used, can produce masks of a professional standard.

1. Exploring Character

For centuries, character masks have been made in the worldwide theatre according to tradition, out of wood, linen, leather and papier-mâché. The character masks of our own European mask tradition, the commedia dell´arte, were made by carving the face in wood and taking a positive mould from this in leather.[1] Today, metal, modern plastics, fibreglass, fabrics, rubber and vinyl silicone are all used and computers, electronics and the science of robotics are also exploited to make masks and models appear more lifelike. We can feast our eyes on the wizardry of television mask-makers, from the pioneer *Sesame Street*, to the BBC's *The Lion, the Witch and the Wardrobe* and more. Special effects, model-making and prosthetic achievements for the film industry are multi-million dollar concerns involving ingenuity, artistry and technology.

The mask-maker often seeks to create recognisable characters and these can take many different forms. Some are grotesque and exaggerated, such as the burlesque masks of the Swiss Carnival. Others are infinitely subtle and refined as, for example, Japanese Noh masks. Mask-makers can base their art on imaginative representation to show gods, demons and spirits; others take from life and turn features into caricature *(figs. 110–111)*.

Physiognomy, or the art of reading character from the face, stems from the time of Ancient Greece, and was practised in Rome and Mediaeval Europe. Basic to physiognomy was the idea that there were four types of face associated with four basic temperaments, or humours: the sanguine, the phlegmatic, the choleric and the melancholic, and that these corresponded to the four elements from which the whole universe was composed: air, water, fire and earth. The humours were also associated with the four chief fluids of the body, namely, blood for sanguine types, phlegm for phlegmatic types, yellow bile for choleric types and black bile for melancholic types.

Fig. 110 *(facing page).* The buck teeth and leering smile of this mask suggest a character associated with low spirits and demons. In a drama he usually represents a demon or aggressive lord. The moustache, hair and brows are made from goat's hair and hide; the teeth are shell. *Balinese. Private collection. 20th century.*

A person's physical and mental qualities were believed to be determined by the relative proportions which they possessed of these four bodily fluids.[2]

Most contemporary evidence shows that we look the way we do because of the infinite variety in the shapes and proportions of the skull, as well as its covering of muscle and skin. In addition, looks are determined by inheritance, environment, and the ageing process.[3] Artists, however, most notably caricaturists and illustrators such as the late Jim Henson, Gerald Scarfe, Quentin Blake, John Burningham, Michael Foreman and Janet Ahlberg, all bring alive their characters by the way they exaggerate their features. In mask-making, many characters from children's books or poetry lend themselves to masked caricature. When making masks, you can have a clear idea of the character type that you wish to portray and work from photographs or sketches, or you can begin to make the mask and allow the character to emerge as you work. With the latter method there is the added benefit that anxiety does not build up as to whether the mask will turn out 'right' and you can see how the character of the mask alters as it 'grows'.

Character mask-making in the theatre often begins at the same unglamorous point. The mask-maker uses the sculptor's technique of taking a cast from the actor's face. This can be done with plaster of Paris, or plaster-impregnated bandage, called Mod-Roc (used to make 'pots' for broken limbs). Another technique, less messy, is moulded paper gum-strip.

Fig. 111. Moulded clay Greek Satyr mask with a bronze-like finish. *The island of Symi. 20th century. Private collection.*

2. Making a Moulded Paper Gum-strip Mask

OBJECTIVES

- Designing and making a mask moulded on the face
- Exploring character
- Designing half- or full-face masks
- Designing and making a mask that is durable
- Designing and making masks suitable for work on commedia dell´arte.

Each person will require:

- One roll of 5cm wide, brown paper gum-strip for tearing into lengths, pieces, etc. (shared between four)

- ☐ Large, soft, paper tissues (large paper handkerchiefs or soft toilet roll)
- ☐ A small amount of thin card or cartridge paper
- ☐ Das modelling material or Plasticine
- ☐ Poster, acrylic or other suitable paints
- ☐ String
- ☐ Scissors
- ☐ Felt-tipped pens
- ☐ Table or desks to lie on
- ☐ A damp sponge in a plastic food container (for dampening the gum-strip)
- ☐ A plastic container for storing torn pieces of gum-strip

Don't forget to tear the gum-strip so that the edges mesh together as you work, and thus create a smooth surface.

●

Making the Mask

Sophisticated masks can be made using this method; because of the materials and techniques involved, it would be preferable to work with small groups of older pupils, students or adults. The form of the mask will be determined by its function and questions should be considered, such as:

Is the mask to be a full-face or a half-face mask?

Does the group have a specific character in mind, for example a proud person or a happy person?

Alternatively, will the group begin by making the mask and simply allow the character to 'emerge'?

To make a brown paper gum-strip mask, follow the guide outlined here or work out your own system on the basis of the materials provided. When working with groups use the following guide to demonstrate how to make a mask, before allowing them to embark on their own mask-making.

i) Partners

Decide who is to be the model and who is the mask-maker. Models should lie on the table and make themselves comfortable, perhaps by putting a jumper or cushion underneath their heads. The subsequent mask forms will belong specifically to each model. Part of the fun of this process is making sure the models remain comfortable and, above all, still and calm throughout!

ii) Prepare the brown paper gum-strip

Tear the brown paper gum-strip into roughly the following lengths: six of 30cm, twenty of 3cm, fifty of 1cm.

〉

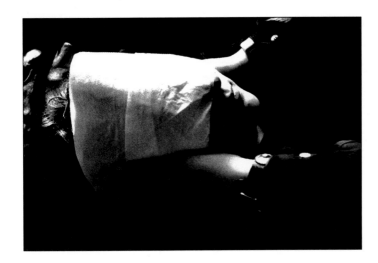

Fig. 112.

Fig. 113.

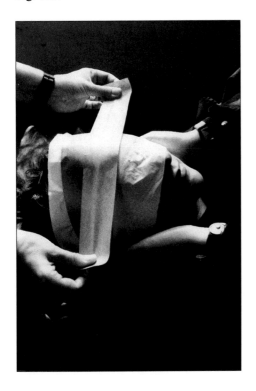

These amounts are only a guide; once one mask is made it is possible to calculate exactly how many pieces will be needed for the next mask. A plastic food container can be used to keep the pieces dry, whilst working.

iii) The three sections of the face

Section 1 is the forehead, section 2 includes the eyes to the tip of the nose, section 3 is the mouth and chin area. First of all cover sections 1 and 2 of the face with soft paper tissue to form a barrier between the wet gum-strip and your model's face *(fig. 112)*.

iv) How to make a half-mask

Dampen one of the 30cm pieces of gum-strip and place it horizontally over the tissue, at the point just below the hairline. Place the second length below this as far as the eyebrows *(fig. 113)*.

Ask the model to hold the paper in place during mask-making *(fig. 114)*.

It is important to press the gum-strip gently to the model's face as you work, so that the gum-strip will retain the shape of the face as it dries.

Next, dampen one 3cm piece of gum-strip and lay it across the bridge of the nose *(fig. 115)*.

Then overlap as many 1cm pieces as are necessary to cover the whole eye area *(fig. 116)*.

Build up no more than two layers of gum-strip at this stage. If a half-mask is required, leave the mask to dry on the model's face for about five minutes at this point, before moving to the finishing off stage.

>

Fig. 114.

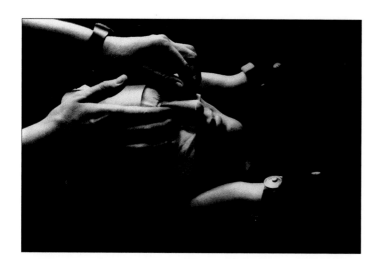

Fig. 115.

Fig. 116.

Fig. 117.

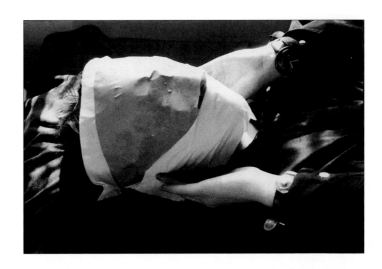

Fig. 118 .

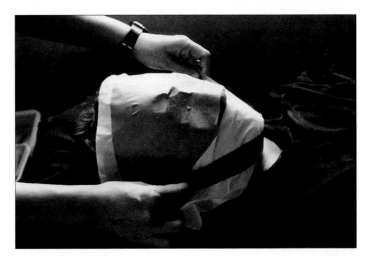

Fig. 119.

v) How to make a full-face mask

To make a full-face mask simply continue the process as follows:

Keeping the nostrils free, cover section 3 of the face with tissue *(fig. 117)*.

Place one 30cm piece of gum-strip under the chin and join it up to both sides of the mask *(fig. 118)*.

Then layer as many 3cm pieces of dampened gum-strip as necessary to cover the entire jaw area. Remember to mould the gum-strip as it dries, by gently pressing it to the shape of the model's face *(fig. 119)*.

Finally, a long piece of gum-strip should be brought round the top of the face *(fig. 120)*.

When the gum-strip mask is dry, remove it from the model's face and either swap roles in order to make another basic gum-strip mask, or move straight onto the finishing off stages with the first mask.

vi) Finishing-off stages

Use sharp scissors to trim the ragged edges of the mask *(figs. 121–122)*.

〉

Fig. 120.

Fig. 122.

Fig. 121.

Fig. 123.

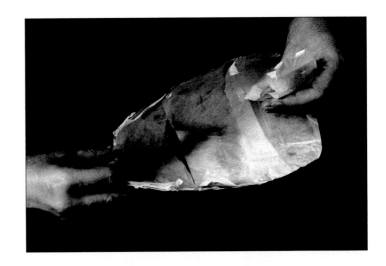

Fig. 124.

Fig. 125.

Remove the tissue from inside the mask by first dampening it
very slightly and then gently rubbing it off with the fingers.
This is done so as to leave the inside of the mask dry and
clean *(fig. 123)*.

Fold paper gum-strip round the edges to neaten them and
to prevent the layers from splitting *(fig. 124)*.

One way to discover where the mask needs strengthening
is to hold it up to the light and add more torn gum-strip
pieces to the places where the light shows through *(fig.
125)*.

Continue to layer 3cm pieces of torn gum-strip over the
mask in order to strengthen it.

〉

vii) Cut out the holes for the eyes and mouth

Hold the mask up to the model's face to determine the position of the eyes and mouth. Draw large eyeholes and, if making a full-face mask, draw a large mouth shape and then cut them out *(figs. 126–128 and 140)*.

>

Fig. 126.

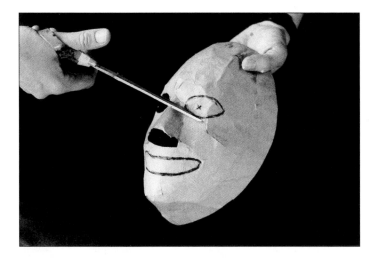

Fig. 127.

Fig. 128.

Fig. 129.

Fig. 130.

viii) Build-up the features

Using the paper-construction method, the card can be torn, cut and manipulated into shapes such as cones, triangles and curves to make the following features:

Eyelids – A strip of card can half-close the eyes, or open them wide. Experiment with its positioning to make dramatic changes to the expression. Make these first, before inserting the eyes.

Eyes – The mask takes on an expression, if 'eyeballs', with the eyes drawn on, are added. Make a slit to see out of, underneath the eye socket. This is a device often used in dance masks, instead of making an eye, the wearer's own eyes can be left to shine through the slit *(fig. 129)*.

›

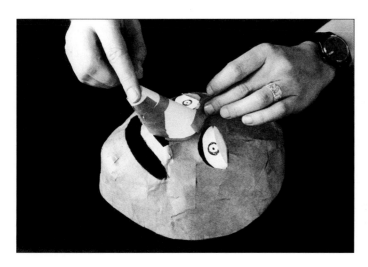

Noses – Experiment with shapes to see what expressions emerge *(fig. 130)*. Keep the nostrils free.

Ears – A simple exercise in symmetry is to make two ears the same *(figs. 131–132)*.

Hair – Is the hairstyle spiky, coiled or curled? What about a fringe or beard?

Teeth – Are they small and pointed or ferocious fangs?

Other features – Wrinkles, warts and tips of noses can be added by using Das or Plasticine. Place a small piece of modelling material onto the mask form and mould into the desired shape. (Do not add too much

〉

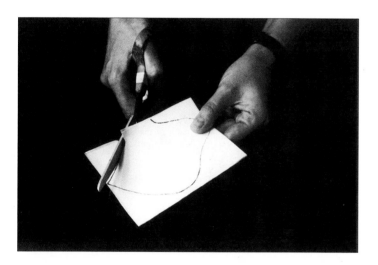

Fig. 131.

Fig. 132.

Fig. 133.

as this will make the mask heavy.) Cover this shape with 1cm pieces of gum-strip. The modelling material can continue to be moulded beneath this before it dries.

ix) *How to ensure that the mask stays lightweight*

If larger amounts of modelling material are used then follow the next procedure in order to ensure the mask remains a lightweight shell structure:

The Das shrinks as it dries, therefore it can be broken up and carefully removed from a gap cut on the inside of the mask. The brown paper gum-strip shell of the mask, which has been layered over the Das, will keep its shape and it is possible to remove all of the modelling material from inside the mask in this way, thus leaving a lightweight shell. Once all the dried modelling material has been removed, the inside of the mask should be re-lined with torn paper gum-strip in order to make it smooth again.

x) *Fitting the mask*

Add the string or elastic which will tie the mask onto the face. This can be knotted through holes at the sides or actually built into the main body of the mask by running it across the inside and then covering it in brown paper gum-strip. Once this point is reached make a checklist to test each mask, for example:

Can the wearer see clearly to the front and to the sides?
Are there any sharp pieces of paper to endanger the face?
Is there room for the nose?
Can the wearer breathe and speak?
Will the mask stay on? *(figs. 133 and 139)*

xi) *Strength and durability*

The making process involves the careful layering of small pieces of torn brown paper gum-strip, which will, eventually create a rock-hard structure. Add the final layers when you are sure the mask is formed. The aim is to create a smooth surface with all the edges of the paper meshed

⟩

Fig. 134. 'The Harpy Eagle', from a series of masks made from paper and coloured fabrics, with matching costumes, representing the animals and birds of the rainforest. *'Yanomamo', a choral work by Rose and Conlon. Costumes by Margaret Ellyard and Viv Peacock. Masks by students at Newland School for Girls, Hull. 1990.*

together, without any sharp edges. Once made, this mask will last. If damaged, paper and glue will repair it. A cloth lining should protect it from the inevitable sweat which builds up behind the mask when worn on stage.

xii) Painting and finishing the mask

There are many ways to finish the masks. The brown paper surface itself can be an effective finish. Simply use colour to highlight the cheeks and nose or darken the shadows. A layer of P.V.A. or good quality varnish will finish and protect the surface.

Coloured paper or pieces of coloured cloth can be stuck to the surface and these can be given a final coating of P.V.A. Masks can be painted in colours symbolic of their meaning or they may be painted in predominantly one colour with the features picked out in other colours. Traditionally the inside of the mask is lined with black felt, or painted matt black. *(figs. 134–135).*

Fig. 135. 'The Sloth'. Dancer wearing a half-mask made from brown paper gum-strip and card decorated with embroidery and a tie-dye costume, both of which she made as an examination project. *'Yanomamo', a choral work by Rose and Conlon, performed by pupils of Newland School for Girls, Hull. 1990.*

ARTS ACTIVITIES

Movement

Basic Physical Warm-up

Working with masks involves using the whole body and often moves are larger than life. Emphasis is put on moving the neck, shoulders and upper body in a more exaggerated manner than normal and therefore, before working with the masks, it is important to relax the whole body and compose the mind. A whole-body warm-up should stretch and flex the body. All moves can be carried out to a count of ten.

Body Stretch

Stand erect with the feet apart. Face forward, keeping a firm stance, but be loose at the knees. You can lead the movement by following this pattern:
>   Stretch both arms up and push up for a count of ten, then lower.
>   Stretch the left arm up, push up for a count of ten, then lower.
>   Stretch the right arm up, push up for a count of ten, then lower.
>   Repeat.

Body Bend

Stand erect with feet apart and body relaxed. Let the head fall forward. Gradually roll the head, neck and back, down as far as you can without straining. Then reverse the movement starting from the base of the spine; gradually roll back up into an upright position.

Body Swing

It is important to do this slowly. Stand with legs apart, clasp the hands and swing the completely relaxed body from side to side like a bell.

Head Roll

Stand in a relaxed manner. Face forward. Allow the head to drop forward, chin down. Slowly tip the head right back while keeping the neck relaxed. Return the head to the upright position. Now tip the head from side to side, first to the right, then to the left, all the time relaxing the neck muscles.

Shoulder Lift

Raise and lower the shoulders, arms hanging loosely. Move the shoulders in a circle. Lift the shoulders in turn. Keeping the arms loose, circle the shoulders in opposite directions.

Wrist and Arms

Circle each wrist in turn, clockwise and anticlockwise, with hand stretched, but arm relaxed. Swing arms together and then in turn, keeping the arms loose so as to allow the lower arm to swing by its own weight.

Ankle and Legs

Circle each stretched foot in turn, holding the thigh horizontal, knee relaxed. Swing each leg in turn, allowing the lower leg to swing by its own weight.

Drama

Masked actors must always be aware of the mask. Even though they cannot see themselves on stage they must always keep a sense of the relation between their movements and the expression of the mask. If the mask 'dies' in performance, then the performers can sense that the audience is no longer with them. When the mask 'works', the audience remain intrigued and entertained. Masked performance is a form of physical theatre; the dramatic focus is more on what the actor does than what is said, so the actor relies on movement, mime and dance techniques rather than verbal wit *(figs. 136 -138)*.

Individual Work

Each performer should spend some time holding the mask out in front of him or herself and looking at it. The masks should not be moved about, but kept still to allow their expressions to be absorbed. Allow the wrist to move the mask, not in a predetermined way, but in an exploratory manner. Notice how the mask changes expression as it moves. Alternatively, performers could wear the masks and look in a mirror; they should not force any movements but allow them to develop gradually through careful observation.

Pair Work

One of the partners should wear the mask and gradually begin to experiment with movements. They should move slowly and start by keeping each movement separate and exaggerated. The other person watches and advises, saying which of the movements is the most effective, because it seems to bring out the character of the mask. Eventually a movement pattern can be built-up which proves the most expressive way of moving when wearing each particular mask.

Building a Character

One partner wears the mask and the other asks questions relating to the mask in order to build-up a 'personal profile' for the mask, for example, 'What is your name, occupation, life history or favourite food?' Also, establish a particular way of walking that is suited to the character of the mask; it might be long, slow strides or short, quick steps.

Focusing

Begin this exercise without the mask in the first instance. Rehearse the technique of focusing, by standing anywhere in the room and fixing your gaze on a particular spot such as a mark on the floor or wall. At the same time, have in mind another place in the room. At a given sound or cue (for example, a hand clap) turn the head to look at the other spot. When wearing a mask, remember that it

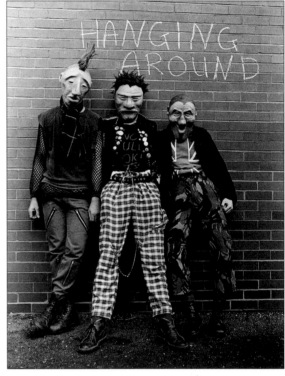

Fig. 136 (*top left*). 'Pierrot' made from paper gum-strip.
Fig. 137 (*lower left*). 'Cat' half-mask made using the torn
paper gum-strip method and Das modelling material.
*Designed and worn by student in mask-making workshop, Hull
Dance Project, Spring Street Theatre. 1989.*
Fig. 138 (*above*). Modern helmet masks made from fibreglass
of three 'Yobs' from Trestle Theatre Company's play *'Hanging
Around'. 20th Century.*

Fig. 139. *Fitting a half-mask of unpainted paper gum-strip.* Adult mask-making workshop, Spring Street Theatre, Hull. 1988.

only works for an audience when the mask is seen from the front or the sides and therefore, it is essential to keep the focus of the mask 'out front' during all movements.

'Shrinking and Growing'

Wear the mask and focus out front. Take a small and withdrawn stance. On a sound cue gradually 'grow' and move forward at the same time. When the movement is complete, withdraw backwards to 'shrink' to the smaller pose. Do not lower the head but keep the mask facing up and out to the front all the time.

Improvising in Pairs or Small Groups

Devise a situation where the masks can meet and interact in order to bring out their character, for example:

'The Cocktail Party'

Two friends are at a cocktail party; they comment on the other guests and gossip. Another friend joins them and the gossip continues. Eventually, all the guests are drawn into the situation.

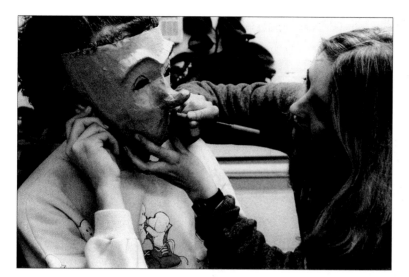

Fig. 140 (*left*). Drawing the mouth on an incomplete paper gum-strip and card character mask.

Fig. 141 & Fig. 142. Improvisations using character masks made from unpainted paper gum-strip and Das modelling material as described in the section on moulded paper gum-strip mask-making. *Adult mask-making workshop, Spring Street Theatre, Hull. 1988.*
Fig. 141 (*left*). 'Tea Party'.
Fig.142 (*following page*). 'Thieves'.

'The Tea Party'

A young man asks his girlfriend round for tea to meet his parents. Mime setting out the tea things and preparing for the visit. When the girl arrives, everything she says and does is a catastrophe *(fig. 141)*.

113

3. Commedia dell'Arte

The masked tradition which has exerted an enormous (often unacknowledged) influence on professional theatre in Europe originates from the sixteenth century Italian commedia dell'arte. As an acting technique it is an exacting discipline involving pace, poise and quick-wittedness in the actor and vitality and economy in the dramatist. Shakespeare used it and built on it; contemporary theatre still thrives on it. The influence of commedia on modern theatrical technique is, generally speaking, unacknowledged. It has been absorbed into the mainstream, passed down as a living tradition from practitioner to practitioner and not necessarily documented.

Inextricable from the commedia acting techniques are the characters and their masks. Harlequin, Pantaloon, Pulchinella, the Doctor and the rest are male archetypes (it seems there were no female masks). Commedia masks are leather half-masks and still made today in the traditional way. These masks are preferred by actors because they are so light and comparatively comfortable. The exact details of the traditional method are only to be discovered by visiting and training with a professional leather mask-maker, and then undertaking to make your own mask, following their methods and learning by trial and error. Here is a very rough guide, which only gives the barest of outlines for this highly specialized technique:

First a correctly proportioned face is modelled out of clay, from which a negative cast is taken in plaster of Paris. A positive cast is then taken (from the negative), again using plaster of Paris. From this positive plaster model, a wooden one is made by first measuring out the proportions of the face and features, and then carving them in wood. Finally, a sheet of good quality leather is pressed over the features of the wooden carving so as to make a positive form. There are so many techniques to be mastered and pitfalls to be avoided along the way to actually making such a mask, that only a 'master' can teach it properly. It is not surprising that many would-be leather mask-makers make the pilgrimage to Italy to seek out such makers as Donato Sartori at the Centro Maschere e Strutture Gestuali.

It is virtually impossible to capture the acrobatic movement and vitality of commedia acting in words. However, descriptions of their characters and favourite antics and 'boasts' have been recorded and these are not only interesting in their own right, but can also form a stimulus for your own work. I can recommend Duchartre's book on the commedia for descriptions of the character masks, their actions, manner of moving and associated scenarios.[4] These certainly knock on the head any idea that masked theatre is always mysterious, vague or fusty *(figs. 143–148)*.

Fig. 143. 'Harlequin': he has many sides to his personality. He can be immensely stupid, yet he is very funny. In performance he is agile, moving like a cat and making jumps and somersaults. *Mike Chase, Mask-maker, London. Private collection. 20th century.*

Fig. 144. 'Pulchinella': better known as Punch, he has a humpback and large nose. He is witty, cruel and two-faced. He walks like a hen, making a 'peeping' sound like a chicken. *Mike Chase, Mask-maker, London. Private collection. 20th century.*

Figs. 143–148. Series of six commedia dell'arte masks.

Fig. 145. 'Zanni': the foolish servant who dithers and is always afraid. *Mike Chase, Mask-maker, London. Private collection. 20th century.*

Fig. 146. 'Pantaloon': old, mean and miserly, he has long legs and likes to wear red trousers. He moves as if he is being followed. *Mike Chase, Mask-maker, London. Private collection. 20th century.*

A Simple Way to Make a Commedia Mask

In the non-specialist workshop or the classroom, the moulded brown paper gum-strip mask-making method described earlier in Project Six, will make effective masks representing commedia characters, especially if combined with paper-construction (see pages 96–109). Although far humbler in technique than the real leather mask-making, these paper gum-strip masks can serve you very well if care is taken when making and finishing them. The photographs included here show the main commedia character masks and could serve as examples for your own mask-making.

ARTS ACTIVITIES

Drama

Once a group of masks has been made, a comic scenario along commedia lines can be devised. Do not restrict yourself to copying the commedia types, but update them and use them as a stimulus for your own ideas. First of all it is essential to study the masks and to formulate a character. Look in a mirror and try different movements and see which ones seem to 'fit' the mask. Often it works best to start by moving very little at all and allow the mask to 'tell' you what to do. Also, work together with a partner and take it in turns to build a character for each other's masks. One wears a mask whilst the other asks them questions such as:

'What is your name?'
'How are you today?'
'What is your favourite food?'
'Have you a job?'

The person wearing the mask replies and moves in character. From then on the two masked characters can work together to improvise a short scene, keeping to the character of the masks.

Status Games

All the masked characters stand in a circle. A command is passed around the group from one to another, for example, 'pass the salt!'. Each masked character tries to 'put down' the other by the superior manner in which he or she speaks and moves.

'Hat'

Half the characters stand in a line and the other half form an audience. The character at the end of the line is proudly wearing a hat. The character immediately next in line looks at it admiringly and then removes it and puts it on his or her own head. The character from whom the hat has been removed then reacts in a manner appropriate to its mask. This is repeated by everyone in the line.

'Newspaper'

Half the group is masked and seated, the rest form their audience. One of the seated group is engrossed in a newspaper. The character immediately next to him or her steals it, and the first character is crushed or incensed by this action. The newspaper works its way along the line. Each character reacts in a way fitting to his or her mask.

'Status'

The higher status characters should think of some tricky or time-wasting tasks for the others to do and issue them as verbal commands, for example:

'You simply must find my pet grass snake!'

'Count the number of hairs on my dog!'

'I've lost the ring that my darling husband gave me – find it!'

'You must remove this ink stain from my best silk pyjamas!'

The other character has to give a suitably humble verbal response. Choose one of the commands and responses and build a scene in which the servant gets everything wrong. Then play the scene again but 'turn the tables' on the master or mistress.

'The Master and the Servant'

Often one mask will appear to be more dominant than another. Allow the dominant mask to take the higher status role or to be the master/mistress to the other's servant. A favourite commedia device is to have the higher status characters adopting different speech patterns as well as different ways of moving, to reflect their higher status, in contrast to their minions. It is amusing if the servant never speaks but simply mimes and obeys the master, conveying his or her feelings through actions alone.

Scenes can be built around ideas which required the master or the mistress to tell the servant what to do. For example, they are the master/mistress and the servant packing for a holiday and one is always giving orders to the other. Or one is eating and the other serving them. Or one is sitting watching the television and constantly demanding that the other runs errands and completes menial tasks. The servant never answers back.

'The Worm Turns'

Play the master/servant scene as above, but gradually allow the servant to take over the master's role in action and dialogue.

Fig. 147. 'Brighella': the most sinister of all the characters. He prowls like a rat and is out to rob and trick. *Mike Chase, Maskmaker, London. Private collection. 20th century.*

Fig. 148. 'Captain': big-mouthed and aggressive, he rolls his R's and likes to march about and stamp. When frightened though, he pretends to be dead. *Mike Chase, Maskmaker, London. Private collection. 20th century.*

Gods, Dragons & Demons

A resource chapter of mask-making ideas for group activities, festivals, parades and plays, for people of all ages

1. Dragons and Other Mythical Creatures

Dragons are some of the finest masked creations of the theatre. They come in every shape and a variety of sizes. They are found in popular and classical theatre in Europe, across India and China, from Indonesia to Australia and throughout Central and South America. They can be seen paraded through modern streets, yet their origins go back to the time of the Bronze Age.[1]

Dragons are ambiguous creatures. On the one hand they can be cruel tormentors of captive maidens, breathing fire and destruction; on the other hand they can be benign bringers of good luck, whose fierce appearance wards off evil spirits. In the West dragons tend to be predators with a predilection for young girls and they are usually harried to death by knights such as St George. In the East, however, they inhabit exotic crystal and coral palaces. They are unpredictable but essential natural forces, stirring up storms and hurricanes; therefore, they are humoured but never destroyed.

It is unwise to be dogmatic about the shape of a dragon, because there are many kinds. Some are snakes or lizards with scaly skins; some have a snake's head, the body of a lion, the legs of a deer, a goat, a ram or a bull. The tail can be that of a lizard, a crocodile, a fish, an eel or a dolphin. Chinese dragons are said to have the head of a camel, the horns of a stag, the eyes of a demon, the ears of a cow, the neck of a snake, the scales of a carp and the claws of an eagle.[2] Identifying dragons is tricky because they are forever transforming themselves. They can make themselves as tiny as baby lizards or as large as clouds. They can be half-human and half-animal like the chimera. They can be spirit and flesh or water and fire. They have alarming habits; for example, snake dragons are forever chasing and swallowing their own tails and falling in love with their own reflections.[3] The dragon snake circle is said to represent time itself and the natural cycle of birth, life and death. Dragons govern both chaos and rebirth and the conflict and fusion between the elements, earth, fire, water and air.[4]

Fig. 149. Chinese dragon embroidered on silk dressing gown. *Hong Kong. Private collection. 20th century.*

119

Dragons are to be seen in street processions or on stage as masks, but they are also turned into ship's bows, door posts, temple roofs, ornaments, brooches, handles and lids. They are painted squirming across walls and ceilings, embroidered on silk, pictured in books and stamped on coins *(fig. 149)*. They are fashioned from any workable material, from paper, cloth, wood or stone to silver, gold, copper and bronze.

The Balinese Barong

One of the finest conceptions of the dragon in theatre is the Balinese Barong. He is benevolent and life-giving and fights the evil witch-figure Rangda. The Barong is four-legged and animated, like a pantomime horse, by two performers hidden inside. The dragon has an elaborate carved wooden mask, with bulging eyes, fierce grin and fangs. The mask has an intricate tooled leather surround and is worn in the front of the first performer's chest. The performer stands behind it and looks, not through its eyes, but over the top, thus giving the Barong its hunched-shoulders appearance. His costume is made of massive swathes of strips of material, fibre or hair. He has a long and magnificent arched tail and 'magic in his beard'.[5]

Fig. 150 *(right)*. Balinese Barong and Monkey sitting on the steps leading to the doorway of Bedulu temple, Southern Central Bali. At the beginning of a secular dance drama, Barong and Monkey are introduced to the audience to display the ability of the dancers in mime, dance, humour and gesture. *Bali. 20th century.*

The Story of Barong and Rangda

Barong-Rangda plays are sacred dramas involving a variety of masked demons and monsters, focusing on Barong, a beneficial lion or dragon, and Rangda, an evil she-devil. The principal theme is the fight between good and evil, dragon and demon.[6] Whatever its details, the story generally follows the same pattern as outlined by this series of photographs taken of a Barong-Rangda performance shown on the steps leading to the doorway of Bedulu temple, Southern Central Bali *(figs. 150–157)*.

Fig. 151 (*left*). Barong grooming himself and showing off to the audience.

Fig. 153 (*below*). Barong and Rangda fight.

Fig. 152 (*above*). Rangda terrorizes the villagers; at this point the performers are in a trance.

Fig. 154 (*right*). The villagers attack Rangda.

Fig. 155. Rangda casts a spell and causes them to turn upon themselves.

Fig. 156. Barong is resurrected.

Fig. 157. A village priest, or Pemangku, blesses the dancers, exorcising the demons that possess them and thereby releasing them from their trance.

Chinese Rain Dragons

Rain dragons emerge in Spring, on the fifteenth day of the first month of the Chinese New Year. A great din is made with fire-crackers and drums in order to wake them from their sleep in their crystal and coral palaces. The dragons have snapping jaws, mon-strous eyes, horns and claws. Their long bodies are supported on poles by young men who run with them held on high, twisting like huge snakes. The dragons are manipulated to dance, rear, entwine each other and fight. They snake around each other then leap away to the sound of firecrackers and flashes, like thunder and lightning.[7]

Fig. 158. Cantonese lion during Chinese New Year celebrations. *Chinese Community Centre, Hull. 1989.*

The Chinese Dancing Lion

Cantonese lions can be found in the streets of Chinese commu-nities all over the world, at the time of the Chinese New Year. These fantastic lions are benevolent bringers of peace and good luck.[8] Their ferocious looks chase devils away. Their jaws move and they are worn by two dancers who drape a loose cloth over their bodies. The masks are made from cane and paper, adorned with fringed whiskers and glass baubles *(fig. 158)*.

The Padstow Old 'Oss

Padstow is a town in Cornwall and the Padstow 'Oss is a cousin of the hobby-horse (linear descendant of a *drac*, or French dragon). It appears on May Day and is one of the great folk characters of

Fig. 159. The Padstow Old 'Oss paraded through the streets of Padstow, Cornwall. *May Day 1990.*

England. Unlike other hobby-horses, the Padstow 'Oss is black. A large circular hoop, covered with black canvas, is supported on the carrier's shoulders and a long skirt hangs down from this to hide the wearer. It looks rather like a large drum. The carrier's head sticks out from the middle of the drum and is covered by a tall conical hat and a fierce looking black and white mask. A horse's head is held out to the front of the carrier and a short tail sticks out from the back. No one knows its precise origins *(fig. 159)*.[9]

Ideas for Making Dragons

i) Problem-solving

A large dragon head can be made by a small group of people, who must ensure enough time is allowed. The group should research their dragon, brainstorm ideas, then make sketches of their proposed dragon head before beginning to make it. They should list the materials needed to construct it and will have the problem of finding the materials and devising techniques allowing them to realize their designs. Encourage individuals in the group to keep a diary, recording the problems encountered at each stage from design through to completion, including any necessary improvisation and modification of ideas.

Specific problems could be posed, for example:

How can you make the jaw move?

〉

How is the head to be carried? Is it supported on the shoulders, or is it held by hand?

Where do the carriers look out from?

How many carriers is the dragon designed for?

How is the rest of the body to be attached to the head?

The finished dragon must be large but lightweight and strong. What kind of materials could it be made from?

What tools will be needed?

What kind of glue and what other fixing-agents will be required?

ii) Decide which tools to use

- ☐ Hammer
- ☐ Pliers and wire-cutters
- ☐ Needles and thread
- ☐ Paint brushes

iii) Make a framework

This might be made from a combination of the following:

- ☐ Basket willows (these should be soaked in water before being bent into curved shapes)
- ☐ Basket cane
- ☐ Garden wire (this bends to any shape)
- ☐ Chicken wire
- ☐ Lightweight wood

iv) Decide on which other materials to collect

- ☐ Cardboard tubes
- ☐ String and tape for binding canes together
- ☐ Latex glue
- ☐ Brown paper gum-strip (torn into strips, pieces)
- ☐ Lightweight paper to cover the framework
- ☐ Cloth torn into 'bandage' strips covered in glue to make a stronger covering
- ☐ Acrylic or other suitable paints

v) Details and features

Scales, fangs and talons can be fashioned from card using paper-construction methods.

Bulging eyes can be made from yoghurt cartons, half-tennis balls or parts of egg cartons.

Lolling tongue – try using cloth-covered foam, backed with paper and covered in latex glue.

Moving jaw – should to be made as two separate parts and a way found to hinge them together, with a pulley-system to make them open and close.

>

Dragon's body – add fringes or swathes of cut cloth or paper that move as the dragon dances. Decide whether the dragon is to be animated like a pantomime horse with two carriers, or to have a long body supported from inside by the whole group, or held in the air on poles.

vi) *Painting and finishing the dragon*

It can be painted in colours determined by the type of dragon, or in any way decided by the group.

●

Fig. 160. Looking into the mouth of a giant dragon head. *Strawberry Fair, Midsummer Common, Cambridge. Summer 1975.*

ARTS ACTIVITIES

Movement, Dance and Procession

Animating the dragon will take time, skill and the ability to work together. Activities can be tried both with and without masks.

Voice and Movement Cues

The group should devise cues or subtle signals to be given on stage between performers, before certain moments or actions that involve acrobatics, or particular responses. The audience should not be aware of the cue, but all the performers should be alert to it. The members of the group agree on a cue (e.g. the leader raising his or her hand). The cues should be as subtle as possible so that members of the audience cannot spot them (e.g. when the leader uses certain agreed facial expressions, the group turns, or the actors throw balls or sticks across to each other). This is great fun and requires concentration.

Music Cues

Percussion or any musical accompaniment can be used to spur the dragon into action. Varying the sounds and instruments alters the expression and speed of the action in an exciting combination of sound and movement.

'Follow My Leader'

The leader is placed at the head of the dragon and the group follows his or her movement as a chain reaction. The leader can also give cues on which the rest of the team have to act.

'Making Waves'

The members of the group stand in a line and join hands with arms outstretched. The person at the end sends a wave movement through their arms and onto the next person. The whole body can also be involved in a rise and fall movement.

'Keep Your Distance'

A regular distance is established between each person in the line (for example, an arm's length). They move at different speeds and at different heights but maintain the distance between the members. This can be tried first with arms joined, then independently.

Circle, Spirals and Curves

It is said that dragons move in curved pathways. Therefore, the group of players that form a dragon's body might join hands and travel along a curved pathway. Set them the task of forming various combinations of line movements (for example, moving in a circle and then breaking to form a spiral). The same movement can be performed at different speeds and levels.

Two Lines

Groups can work out floor patterns which involve the weaving and crossing of two lines of people. They should vary the speed and height of the lines and bring two lines together to fight, taunt or ignore each other.

Processions

Presenting a dragon in a procession requires a good team in which everyone can work together with direction from a leader. Untuned percussion can make a musical accompaniment. A procession can be led by a dragon. Avoid routes with too many steps! Plan the route to allow for stops when the play is acted out and the dragon performs a comic interlude, a dance or a fight with the demon. Present the play at one stop and then move on to the next.

2. Demons

Unlike dragons, demons are usually evil. They exist to plague, harass and torment humanity. They are malignant spirits; inferior divinities who bring sickness and psychological torment. In early rituals men, women and children sought to mediate between the world of the spirits and the members of their community through masks and dances. Every unexpected event brought with it fear of the unknown and of magic rites. Sacred ceremonies were instituted to avert evil and encourage good.[10] Occasions such as birth, puberty, marriage, war, death, changes of season, hunting and harvest were among those celebrated by dance and ritual, and masks were made to represent the forces of evil that lurked within every aspect of life *(fig. 161)*.

In Sri Lanka there are demon dance ceremonies whose aim is to cure ailments said to have been caused by demons such as earache or vomiting. Shamans impersonate the demons through any one of the eighteen different masks that they wear.[11]

Lucifer

In Medieval Europe, the Christian liturgy was acted out at Easter, in the form of Mystery Plays, which can be seen in modern day revivals in England as the York, Wakefield, Lincoln and Chester Mystery Cycles. These plays have innumerable small scenes making up the play-cycle, including *Adam and Eve, Heaven and Hell, Bethlehem and the Nativity, The Massacre of the Innocents, The Crucifixion, The Resurrection* and *The Last Judgement*. Always the greatest comic character, along with Herod, is Satan himself with his team of devils. Satan and his demons are always masked, with horns and animal heads reminiscent of the ancient classical masks. These devils shovel souls into a demonic mask-like hell mouth, which belches smoke as it opens and closes and sometimes takes up to seventeen men to work. The masked demons are also acro-

bats and comics and intrude into other scenes to provide comic light relief.[12]

Imps and Devils

A good example of what is said to be an imp can be found as a carved stone corbel beside the priest's door in the north-east corner of the choir aisle of St Mary's Church, Beverley, England. This type of demon is said to have delighted in playing tricks on the clergy. He would ring the bell calling the faithful at the wrong times or he would blow out the candles in the middle of a sermon. Never dangerous but always irritating, he could be relied upon to make life that

Fig. 161. A large and heavy Sri-Lankan demon mask which takes the shape of a wooden panel carved in relief, in the centre of which is a figure of Maha-Kola Sanniya, leader of all the eighteen Sanni demons (spirits of illness) that flank both sides of the main figure. These masks, although too heavy to wear, are paraded at ritual dances connected with the exorcism of evil spirits that cause illnesses. *Rijksmuseum voor Volkenkunde, Leiden, The Netherlands. Date unknown.*

little bit more difficult by causing minor mishaps. A modern day imp might alter your alarm clock, burn the toast, blow the fuse and hide keys or spectacles *(figs. 162–163)*.

3. Traditional Dragon and Demon Stories

These stories, like that of the battle between the Balinese Barong and Rangda, are typical tales of good versus evil. Such stories might stimulate ideas for street plays and events based on folk traditions and could be adapted to suit modern themes.

'Dragon's Tears'

There is a Chinese folk legend which explains how twenty-four lakes in Szechwan came to be called 'Dragon's Tears': A poor boy caught a fish, but let it go when it begged for its life. As a reward the fish gave the boy a pearl, which brought him and his mother great prosperity. One day, some farmers, curious to find out the reason for the boy's new found wealth, demanded that he hand over the pearl, but he chose to swallow it instead. He was at once transformed into a huge dragon, which rose to the clouds dropping twenty-four tears of farewell to his mother. More folk tales and descriptions of Chinese dragons can be found in Maguerite Fawdry's book *Chinese Childhood*.[13]

'Saint George'

Fig. 162 *(above)*. Carved stone corbel, said to be an imp. *East end of the north aisle of the choir, St Mary's Church, Beverley, East Riding of Yorkshire, England. 14th century.*

Fig. 163 *(below)*. Red devil, carved and painted wood, sitting on the roof of No. 8, North Bar Without. *Beverley, East Riding of Yorkshire. England. Late 19th century.*

Western dragons are often found in heroic tales based on the story of St George. Here the fierce snake-dragon threatens the town and is appeased by the sacrifice of a beautiful maiden. This barbaric act is stopped by St George, who slays the dragon and rescues the maiden, whom he marries. There are numerous folk dragons in France who also have a taste for young girls. Such stories date back to times when wild beasts were actually kept at bay by the superstitious sacrifice of young children. The ending of such ritual practices was rationalised in terms of the killing of the dragon, so the story continues in the form of a gruesome fairy tale or folk legend.[14]

Mummer's Plays

Mummer's plays are spontaneous folk events performed in Winter, particularly at Christmas, and also Easter, throughout the British Isles. By 1950 they had all but died out and only about twelve examples survive as organised events. All the costumes are essentially disguises, because a performer being recognised breaks the luck associated with the event. The mummers wear old coats and hats, covered from top to toe with strips of newspaper and crêpe paper streamers. Most carry wooden swords and props, such as paper crowns and hats, appropriate to their character. All the stories are variations of hero-and-challenger plot-lines and include characters such as St George, King George, Father Christmas or Jan and Bet in a tangle of action that can become incomprehensible. The words of the play are declaimed in rhyming couplets; usually they make little sense. The under-

Ideas for Making Imps and Demon Masks

The moulded paper gum-strip technique described in *Character and Commedia* can be used to make imps and demons *(fig. 164)*.

Fig. 164. Demon mask made from paper gum-strip, designed and worn by a student. *Mask-making workshop led by the author, Hull Dance Project, Spring Street Theatre, Hull. 1988.*

lying themes are life, death and resurrection, but the primitive symbolism of the plays has been corrupted over the centuries into harmless nonsense.[15]

4. Gods and Spirits of Nature

The gods are thought to rule the lives of men, causing illness and death. These need to be countered by invoking through mask, chant, trance and ceremony those powers or aspects of the gods who rule the good, life-giving forces, harmonious integration with the forces of nature being the greatest aim of the tribal religions.[16] The function of the shaman, or holy man, is to mediate between the world of the spirits, the ancestors, animals and nature. As a healer and a prophet the shaman calls upon spirits both good and destructive, which when acted out, take on a very dramatic form. Masks are worn to represent the gods in all their different manifestations.

Cultures throughout the world maintain similar beliefs. Often they are modified in response to changes in habit, or integrated with other religions and customs as they come under the influence of different or more dominant cultures. In modern-day Mexico, a vast country approximately the size of Europe, where, although the dominant language is Spanish, the people speak fifty-seven different Indian languages, the Pre-Hispanic and Occidental images in the fiestas and rituals have become interwoven and cannot be distinguished from each other.[17] In

Fig. 165 (*below*). 'Deer', a Walu mask of carved and painted wood. *Dogon, Mali, West Africa. Private collection. 20th century.*

Fig. 166 (*right*). Seated Dogon figure in 'Lizard' mask and costume. *Museum voor Volkenkunde, Rotterdam, The Netherlands. 20th century.*

132

other cultures, the old rituals survive virtually intact; for example, the Dogon people of West Africa perform spectacular leaping dances in masks and costumes, which represent every aspect of the world they know, from animals, plants and houses to people from other tribes. These survive because the hostile desert environment, surrounded by mountains which are virtually inaccessible, has kept the Dogon largely free from outside influences, although this is becoming increasingly under threat *(figs. 17, 18, 165 and 166).*[18]

Guardian Deities of Tibet

In the Tibetan *Cham*, or mystery plays, monks wearing masks of guardian deities and gods leave the mountains and take part in masked rituals. These rituals and beliefs are as important to the society's well-being, as they are to its agriculture and economy *(fig. 167).*[19]

Dionysus – God of Nature

Dionysus is an ancient Greek cult god of nature and the wilderness, a half-bearded man, half-horned bull, and ancestor of the great Greek theatre masks. His is the oldest type of Greek mask, an image of a river source god. Although used in early Greek theatre to act out the myths of Dionysus, masks of the god were also hung in woods, fields and shrines, as objects of ritual and worship, symbolic of the great mysteries of the wilderness and nature *(fig. 168).*[20]

The Wild Man of Bavaria

Masked wild men, relics of primitive male secret society members, are said to charge through villages in Bavaria, on the eve of St Nicholas' Day, 6 December. Their masks have horns and antlers and they wear massive costumes of animal skins. Their function is close to that of a clown. They invoke ideas of the wilderness and fertility, and their main occupation is to go from house to house, chasing the women and promising them children. Although they can be frightening they are also seen as bringers of good luck.[21]

The Green Man

Look up at the stone carvings on old cathedrals and churches and you will sometimes find a representation of the Green Man, with leaves and branches issuing from his face. The first representation of him is as a head formed with leaves in Roman art of the first century A.D., and later on he became absorbed into Christian imagery. The Green Man is the complementary figure to the Earth Goddess, or Mother Nature; he represents male creativity and the male aspects of nature. In the English medieval poem *Sir Gawain and the Green Knight* he submits the hero to challenge death. In English folk stories he is known as Jack-in-the-Green or Robin Hood and in revivals of May Day festivals he will appear as a man covered in burrs or leaves. Giuseppe Arcimboldo's *The Four Seasons*, painted in the sixteenth century are close to the idea of

Fig. 167 (*above*). Mask of the Tibetan Protector Deity. *Museum voor Volkenkunde, Rotterdam, The Netherlands. Date unknown.*

Fig. 168 (*below*). Fired clay mask of a modern Dionysus. *Sicily. Private collection. 20th century.*

Fig. 169 (*left*). Green Man. *Carved stone capital. Nave Arcade, Beverley Minster, East Riding of Yorkshire. England. 14th century.*
Fig. 170 (*right*). Green Man mask made from wire, cloth and papier-mâché for a performance of the opera *Sir Gawain and the Green Knight* by Harrison Birtwhistle. *Jocelyn Herbert, Designer. 20th century.*

the Green Man. Today he might be found taken on as a symbol of the Green Movement. In Norway, for example, the Green Man has been adopted as a symbol of nature under threat from acid rain *(figs. 169–171)*.

FURTHER READING FOR MYTHS

- Cotterell, Arthur, *The Illustrated Encyclopedia of Myths and Leg-ends* (Cassell, London, 1992, & Macmillan, New York, 1989).
- Hughes, Ted, *Tales of the Early World* (Faber & Faber, London, 1988, Farrar, Strauss, & Giroux, New York, 1989).
- Jones, Terry, *Fairy Tales* (Puffin Books, London & New York, 1987).
- Jordan, Michael, *Encyclopedia of Gods* (Kyle Cathie Ltd, London, 1992, & Facts on File, Winchester, Mass., 1993).
- Maclagan, David, *Creation Myths* (Thames & Hudson, London, & New York, 1977).
- O'Brien, Edna, *Tales for the Telling* (Pavilion Books, London, 1986 & Puffin Books, New York, 1988).
- Parrinder, Geoffrey, *African Mythology* (Newnes Books, 1984, & Peter Bedrick Books, New York, 1991).
- Slattum, Judy, *Masks of Bali* (Chronicle Books, San Francisco, 1992). (Available in UK).
- Willis, Roy, (ed) *World Mythology* (Duncan Baird Publishers, 1993, & Henry Holt, New York, 1993).

Fig. 171 (*facing page*). Fired clay mask of Green Man. *Walter Storey, Artist. Private collection. 20th century.*

Masquerade

More mask-making techniques

The techniques outlined here employ relatively simple substances such as papier-mâché and clay, and are suitable for all age groups from ten years upwards. But plaster of Paris, fibreglass and more hazardous materials appropriate only to specialist workshops and adult groups are also discussed.

The idea of a masquerade holds a strong attraction for people of all ages; it is an event at which we create our own characters, the products of myth and imagination *(fig. 172)*. All the projects in this book can provide ideas, characters and mask-making methods for masquerade and make-believe; however, in this section I have included some of those techniques which require more specialized materials and workshop space, if available. I have listed materials, but it is impossible to mention everything that might be needed. At all times you must take note of all instructions which come with the products. Suppliers can be found in the *Yellow Pages* of telephone directories.

Masquerade and History

In eighteenth-century England masquerading was enthusiastically pursued at exclusive gatherings of the aristocracy and people of fashion because they afforded opportunities for ostentatious displays of wealth, a permanent record of which was kept by commissioned costume portraits. The excesses of such gatherings were lampooned at the time by painters such as Hogarth, and writers such as Pope and Fielding. Masquerading as a public event, in parks and specially designed halls, also enabled the social classes in England to mix with each other. The fact that this happened, no matter how fleetingly, provided a safety valve against the polarization of the classes and possible revolution. Such social mixing was unheard of in France.[1]

Research into masquerading, so popular with the aristocracy in eighteenth-century England, will provide an insight into the social and political intricacies of the time. George II and Horace Walpole were confirmed masqueraders and there was much controversy between the Court and the Church about the alleged public immorality at such gatherings. The costumes and masks reflect the increasing opportunities for travel, as many of the masqueraders appeared in Turkish, Persian or Chinese dress.[2]

Fig. 172 *(facing page)*. Red demon. Giant helmet mask constructed from fibreglass paraded at the Notting Hill Carnival, *London. 1992.*

Today the tradition flourishes in Italy, fostered by the economics of the tourist industry. Masks are worn for the Venetian Carnival festivities and the finest of these are handmade by traditional methods and accompanied with elaborate costumes. Venetian half-masks are called *gnaga*, or *larva (fig. 30)*. These are usually white and highly stylized. There are also smaller masks of black velvet, called *moreta*. White lace is traditionally added to the edge of the mask in order to conceal the lower part of the face. The full costume is completed by a large black cloak, called a *domino*, and a piece of black lace or silk called a *bauta* which covers the lower jaw.[3] Mardi Gras, the day before Lent begins, is celebrated in parts of Germany by masked carnival, and masked processions also occur in Switzerland, France and Austria.[4]

Masquerade and Dance

In the sophisticated modern context of the masquerade it is the half-mask that is most frequently used. Such masks, worn at a formal dance or ball, originally gave the guests an opportunity to escape their social identity and play games of assumed roles and mystery. This context is transferred to the theatre in Verdi's opera *Un Ballo in Maschera* and Prokofiev's ballet *Cinderella*, where it offers the director opportunities for lavish masks and costume and spectacular choreography.

Masquerade and Society

Fig. 173. Mask with Constructivist icon, made from paper, designed and worn by an undergraduate student. *'Ice-breaker' workshop led by Richard Penton, Hull School of Architecture. Autumn 1983.*

Social and informal gatherings of many kinds can lend themselves to the wearing of masks. Political leaders, ideologies and even artistic movements have been and are satirized by the wearing of masks *(fig. 173)*. Some of the easiest to wear are traditional half-masks, and guests might be invited to attend wearing a mask based on a given theme. Choose a theme appropriate to the age-range, for example, young children may enjoy making and wearing animal masks. For older children or adults, fancy dress parties can be based on the dress of the past, for example Victorian evenings or Medieval banquets. Other themes might be characters from a book, film or history. Fancy dress costumes and masks provide opportunities to test ingenuity and imaginative improvisation in the use of materials.

STREET THEATRE

Permission must be asked of the local city or county council and police before street performances can be organized, and some cities have specially designated areas where this kind of activity is permitted. Quite often areas of a street are owned by certain shops or companies and it is essential to have their permission before planning a route.

Fig. 174. Actor in street theatre, wearing moulded half-mask of papier-mâché. *Groningen, The Netherlands. Summer 1996.*

Open-air theatre can take place with the action raised on lorries or scaffold platforms, often the outside of churches or the walls of a ruin can make a suitable back-cloth or stage area. More formally organized events, such as those in parks and gardens, require the erection of seating. An amphitheatre arrangement with the audience raised and so looking down on the action is usually preferred. Of course the weather cannot be planned ahead! Street theatre is often arranged as theatre-in-the-round *(fig. 174)*, or with the audience forming a half-moon in front of the action. It is advisable to have a means of drawing the attention of passers-by, for example, with a loud-voiced herald or loud drumming. Preparation is always difficult in public, so if possible the play should be staged in front of the doors of an open building where the inside could be used as the dressing-room and the outside as the stage area. Or choose a building with steps, on which to stage the action. A bandstand is often a good acting area that might have electric sockets, but it is rarely a place to keep the props and costumes.

When devising a street theatre play keep the action very simple. The lines are more effective if declaimed and there is little point in working on subtle characterization. Vary the type of character for the sake of your audience. Characters in mask or on stilts, hobby-horses and jugglers all add variety. It is usually impossible to hear all that is going on unless you use microphones and amplification (not that the audience usually minds if there is enough to look at).

MORE TECHNIQUES FOR MASK-MAKING

Both the brown paper gum-strip and paper-construction techniques outlined in this book can be used to make masks suitable for masquerade. Such masks could range from simple symmetrical paper masks to elaborate paper-construction masks. Ideas for wearing masks might be taken from the theatre costumier, for example a small mask can be held on a stick in front of the face, or if the mask is to be worn, loops of elastic can be put round the ears to hold the mask in place. Lace or ribbons can be used to edge a small mask and add more mystery to the disguise.

Papier-mâché

Papier-mâché is often the material which first comes to mind when mask-making, though some people find it of limited value because it can take too long to dry. However, the very fine and sophisticated masks seen in Venice are made by this technique *(figs. 175–176)*. Each mask-maker will keep his or her method a carefully guarded secret, but often they are variations of the following techniques. You will need:

- ☐ Torn, rather than cut newspaper or plain paper. (Torn edges mesh together when the paper is layered, thus creating a smooth surface.)
- ☐ Torn tissue paper or blotting-paper for the final layers
- ☐ Wallpaper paste made according to the instructions or P.V.A. glue
- ☐ Petroleum jelly as a separator
- ☐ Other materials depending on the choice of base and finishes

The papier-mâché masks can be fashioned on different bases or moulds. For example:

Fig. 175. Venetian carnival masks, made of papier-mâché finished in gold. *Shop window, Groningen, Holland. Summer 1996.*

Clay

Clay can be modelled into a face and papier-mâché layered over this, using petroleum jelly to prevent the paper sticking to the clay and putting torn tissue, or blotting-paper over the top as the final layer. Leave to dry before removing the papier-mâché shell.

Plaster of Paris

A more sophisticated way is to take a plaster of Paris cast of the face,

Fig. 176. 'Sun King', performance artist. *Outside Rijksmuseum, Amsterdam. Summer 1996.*

which has first been modelled in clay, and when the resultant negative mould is removed from the clay, papier-mâché can be layered inside it to take an impression of the face. An initial layer of blotting-paper or tissue paper will give the surface a smoother finish. Use petroleum jelly as a separator throughout the process. These masks can be finished by layering paint and P.V.A. glue or varnish. Experiment with different surfaces, such as gold or silver spray paint. The finished mask can be painted black inside.

Balloons

Balloons are sometimes used as bases and papier-mâché applied. These do not make naturalistic masks but are simple to make and can be effective clown faces or cartoon masks.

Casting a Face

Another method is to take a cast of a live model's face using plaster of Paris. This must only be done with adults, the model wearing protective clothing, a bathing cap and cloth eye covers to safeguard eyelashes and brows. They should lie down facing upwards and their face should be well smeared with petroleum jelly. Straws are put in the nostrils and mouth to allow breathing as the plaster of Paris dries. Mixed plaster of Paris is carefully poured over the face. Once the plaster of Paris is dry it can be removed as a whole piece; inside will be a negative impression of the model's features. I can vouch for the fact that being a model for this process is both uncomfortable and unnerving!

Before working on the mould, some means of support has to be found. A box of sand into which the mould can be carefully pressed, is one way. The negative mould can be used to make positive casts of the model's face by layering papier-mâché inside as described on page 141. The resultant mask can then be finished by layering paint and P.V.A., allowing the layers to dry between applications. Any object, pre-modelled or sculpted, can be reproduced in this way.

Mod-Roc

Mod-Roc* is fabric reinforced plaster which can be purchased from hospital suppliers and used to make a cast of a person's face. The cast itself can be fashioned into a mask, or it can be used as a negative mould to cast from. You will need:

- ☐ Mod-Roc
- ☐ Petroleum jelly
- ☐ Water
- ☐ A bathing cap to fit the model
- ☐ Two circles of cloth to cover the eyes and eyebrows
- ☐ Towel or similar to protect the model's clothes
- ☐ Plenty of newspaper

The model puts on the bathing cap, makes sure his or her clothing is protected and should lie flat and face upwards. The petroleum jelly is applied to the face and two circles of cloth placed over the eyes and eyebrows. The strips of Mod-Roc should be applied so as to completely cover the model's face and be moulded round the features. Care must be taken to leave the model's nostrils free. When dry the whole mask should be re-

Fig. 177. Carnival mask for Ashlyn. Painted Mod-Roc. *Miranda Gray, Artist, Copenhagen, Denmark. 20th century.*

moved carefully. Now the eyes, mouth and nostrils can be cut out and re-shaped, then string or tape attached to the mask through holes either side at ear level.

Another method involves using the Mod-Roc cast of the model's face as a mould. Smear petroleum jelly inside the mask and pour made-up plaster of Paris into it. When dry, the plaster of Paris mask can be removed to form a facsimile of the model's head.

Alternatively, papier-mâché can be applied to the inside of the Mod-Roc mask. Again use petroleum jelly as a separator. (The first layer of paper in the mould should be of torn tissue, or blotting-paper). A lightweight facsimile mask will result which can be finished off and painted *(fig. 177)*.

Large Papier-mâché Heads

A clean plastic rubbish bag filled with old newspapers will form a base on which to fashion the features of a large carnival mask head. First of all cover the newspaper-filled bag with layers of strips of glued paper, next construct the features from card and tape them onto the filled bag. When the paper is dry, remove the old newspapers from inside the head, and paint or finish the head as desired.

Large Fibreglass Heads

In a well ventilated theatre or art workshop (not a classroom) it is possible to make a lightweight but durable mask from fibreglass. You will need:

- ☐ A polystyrene head (as used to support wigs)
- ☐ Modelling clay
- ☐ Fibreglass kit and instructions
- ☐ Lots of old newspapers
- ☐ Rubber gloves and protective clothing
- ☐ Good ventilation

Decide on the features of the mask and model these in clay onto the face of the polystyrene head. Follow the instructions for mixing the fibreglass, cover the clay with this mixture and allow it to dry near an open window. The resultant fibreglass mask has to be sanded and painted before it can be used. Remember to leave eyeholes, nostrils and an opening for the mouth as you work the fibreglass *(fig. 178)*.

Fig. 178 *(facing page)*. Giant fibreglass mask of a head supported on bamboo poles. *Eeyore Children's Festival, Prospect Park, Brooklyn, New York. 1973.*

FURTHER READING ON MASK-MAKING TECHNIQUES

Techniques using paper and found materials:

- Alkema, Chester J., *Mask Making* (Sterling, London, 1988, & New York, 1971).
- Grater, Michael, *Complete Book of Paper Mask-Making* (Dover, London & New York, 1998).

Techniques for theatre design and performance arts.

- Bruun-Rasmussen, Ole and Petersen, Grete, *Make-Up, Costumes and Masks for the Stage* (Sterling, New York, 1982).
- Govier, Jacquie, *Create your own Stage Props* (A. and C. Black, London, 1984, & Prentice Hall, Englewood Cliffs, NJ, 1984).
- Holt, Michael, *Stage Design and Properties Vols. 1 and 2* (Phaidon Press, London, 1993), & *Vol. 1* (Chronicle Books, San Francisco, 1995), & *Vol. 2* (Schirmer Books, New York, 1991).

Techniques involving constructing, casting and carving using a variety of materials, e.g. plaster, wood, leather, Mod-Roc and papier-mâché:

- Beecroft, Glyniss, *Carving Techniques* (Batsford, 1976), & *Casting Techniques* (Charles Scribner's Sons, New York, 1981).
- Coult, Tony and Kershaw, Baz, (eds.), *Engineers of the Imagination* (Methuen, London, 1983, & Heinemann, New York, 1983).
- Dohler, Don (ed.), *Film Magic: The Fantastic Guide to Special Effects Film-making* (Cinema Enterprises, Baltimore, 1984).
- McKay, Glynn, *Mask-Making* (Grange Books, London, 1994 & Book Sales, New York, 1994).
- Sartori, Donato and Lanata, Bruno, *Maschera e Maschere* (La Casa Usher, Florence, 1984).

Epilogue

In this book I have not attempted to offer an anthropological account of different mask-making cultures or to cover all possible mask-making techniques. My aim is to encourage people of all ages to explore their own powers of mask-making, using practical activities which I have developed over time. There are no blueprints or patterns, because each mask is a unique personal expression.

I have always found masks to offer an unexpectedly rich and varied source of creative and educational stimuli, but this is not really surprising. Making a mask is a primary creative act and there are few societies in which masks have played no part. Recent western culture has largely neglected the mask. I hope that this book makes a difference to the way they are regarded. Perhaps in our post-colonial and post-modern age it is time to blow away the dust of superstition, which all too often contaminates our appreciation of masks, and rediscover their life-enhancing potential.

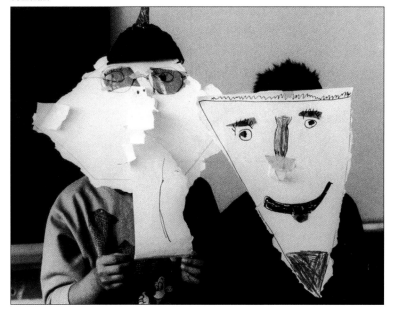

Fig. 179. Two shape-masks. *Designed and worn by pupils in mask-making workshop led by the author, Grange First School, Grimsby, North Lincolnshire. 1989.*

Notes

Introduction

1. Napier, David A., *Masks, Transformation and Paradox*, p. 27.
2. Crocker, J. C., 'Ceremonial Masks', *Celebration: Studies in Festivity and Ritual*, p. 84.
3. Heyneman, Janet, 'Travelling Songs, Waiting Songs', *Parabola* Vol. XIV, No. 1, pp. 35–42.
4. Jenkins, Ron, 'Two-Way Mirrors', *Parabola* Vol. VI, No. 3, pp. 17–21.
5. Brook, Peter, 'Lie and Glorious Adjective', *Parabola* Vol. VI, No. 3, pp. 60–73.

What are Masks?

1. Liggett, John, *The Human Face*, p. 163.
2. *ibid.*, p. 165.
3. Andrews, Carol, *Egyptian Mummies*, p. 27.
4. Miller, Mary Ellen, *The Art of Mesoamerica from Olmec to Aztec*, p. 72.
5. Andrews, Carol, *ibid.*
6. Napier, David A., *Masks, Transformation and Paradox*, p. 3.
7. *ibid.*, p. 7.
8. Miller, Mary Ellen, *op. cit.*, p. 165.
9. Shelton, Anthony, 'Realm of the Fire Serpent', *The British Museum Society Bulletin* No. 98, p. 24.
10. Westendorf, Wolfhart, *Painting, Sculpture and Architecture of Ancient Egypt*, p. 214.
11. Phillips, Tom (ed.), *Africa: The Art of a Continent*, p. 98.
12. Pern, Stephen, *Masked Dancers of West Africa: The Dogon*, p. 94.
13. Goonatilleka, M. H., *Masks of Sri Lanka*, p. 3.
14. Mellors, M., *et al.*, *Masks*.
15. Aris, Michael, 'Sacred Dances of Bhutan', *Natural History*, pp. 38–47.
16. Keene, Donald, *Noh: The Classical Theatre of Japan*, p. 68.
17. Nishikawa, Kyotaro, *Bugaku Masks*, p. 21.
18. Luthra, Chandni (ed.), 'The Folk Theatre of India', p. 2.
19. Bancroft-Hunt, Norman, and Forman, Werner, *People of the Totem*, pp. 86–89.
20. Bieber, M., *The History of the Greek and Roman Theatre*, pp. 81–86.
21. Duchartre, Pierre Louis, *The Italian Comedy*, pp. 24–29.
22. Mack, John (ed.), *Masks: The Art of Expression*, p. 157.
23. *ibid.*, p. 156.
24. Brook, Peter, 'Lie and Glorious Adjective', *Parabola* Vol. V1, No. 3, pp. 60–72.
25. Bihalji-Merin, Oto, *Masks of the World*, p. 98.
26. *ibid.*, p. 99.
27. *ibid.*, pp. 101–102.
28. Goonatilleka, M. H., *op. cit.*, p. 3.
29. *ibid.*, p. 8.
30. Jenkins, Ron, 'Two-Way Mirrors', *Parabola* Vol. VI, No. 3, p. 17.

Masks as Resources

1. Paolozzi, Eduardo, *Lost Magic Kingdoms*, p. 17.
2. Reeve, John, 'Multi-Cultural Work at the British Museum', *Journal of Education in Museums* No. 7, p. 27.
3. Geertz, C., *The Interpretation of Cultures*, p. 5.
4. Willet, Frank, *African Art*, p. 169.
5. The NCC Arts in Schools Project Team, *The Arts 5/16: Practice and Innovation*, p. 115.

Project 5: Theatre, Mask and Myth

1. Gill, Sam, 'It's Where You Put Your Eyes', *I Become Part of It*, pp. 75–87.
2. Stanley, Nick, 'The Unstable Object: Reviewing the Status of Ethnographic Artefacts', *Journal of Design History*, 2.2 and 3, p. 107.
3. Calder, Jenni, *Masks of the Northwest Coast Indians*, Leaflet 7.
4. Lévi-Strauss, Claude, *The Way of the Masks*, pp. 26–27.

Project 6: Character & Commedia

1. Duchartre, Pierre Louis. *The Italian Comedy*, p. 49.
2. Onions, C. T. (ed.), *The Shorter Oxford English Dictionary on Historical Principles* Vol. A–M, p. 933.

Bibliography

3. Liggett, John, *The Human Face*, p. 229.
4. Duchartre, Pierre Louis, *op cit.*, pp. 123–250.

Project 7: Gods, Dragons and Demons

1. Huxley, Francis, *The Dragon*, p. 26.
2. *ibid.*, p. 87.
3. *ibid.*, p. 6.
4. *ibid.*, p. 7.
5. Southern, Richard, *The Seven Ages of the Theatre*, p. 77.
6. *ibid.*, p.77.
7. Fawdry, Marguerite, *Chinese Childhood,* p. 28.
8. Steele, Philip, *Festivals around the World*, pp. 18–19.
9. Shuel, Brian, *The National Trust Guide to Traditional Customs of Britain*, pp. 26–27.
10. Wosien, Maria-Gabriele, *Sacred Dance*, p. 16.
11. Goonatilleka, M. H., *Mask and Mask Systems of Sri Lanka*, pp. 70–71.
12. Hartnoll, Phyllis, *A Concise History of the Theatre*, p. 46.
13. Fawdry, Marguerite, *op cit.*, p. 24.
14. Huxley, Francis, *op cit.*, p. 15.
15. Southern, Richard, *op cit.*, pp. 45–61.
16. Wosien, Maria-Gabriele, *op cit.*, p. 18.
17. Ziff, Trisha, *Between Worlds: Contemporary Mexican Photography*, p. 14.
18. Pern, Stephen, *Masked Dancers of West Africa: The Dogon*, p. 14.
19. Rawson, Philip, *Sacred Tibet*, p. 28.
20. Kerenyi, C., 'Man and Mask', *Spiritual Disciplines: Papers from the Eranos Year Book 4*, p. 157.
21. Southern, Richard, *op cit.*, p. 37.

Project 8: Masquerade

1. Fox, Celina and Ribeiro, Aileen, *Masquerade*, p. 6.
2. Jarvis, Anthea, and Raine, Patricia, *Fancy Dress*, p. 13.
3. Fox, Celina and Ribeiro, Aileen, *op cit.*, p. 7.
4. Bihalji–Merin, Oto, *Masks of the World*, p. 99.

Anderson, W., *Green Man: The Archetype of our One-ness with the Earth* (Collins, London, and Harper, San Francisco, 1990).

Andrews, Carol, *Egyptian Mummies* (British Museum Publications, London, and Harvard University Press, Cambridge, Mass., 1984).

Aris, Michael, 'Sacred Dances of Bhutan', *Natural History* (March, 1980), pp. 38–46.

Bancroft-Hunt, Norman, and Forman, Werner, *People of the Totem* (Orbis, London, and University of Oklahoma Press, Norman, 1985).

Bieber, M., *The History of the Greek and Roman Theatre* (Princeton University Press, NJ, 1961).

Bihalji-Merin, Oto, *Masks of the World* (Thames and Hudson, London, 1971).

Brook, Peter, 'Lie and Glorious Adjective', in Dooling, D.M. (ed.), *Parabola, Vol. VI, No. 3: Mask and Metaphor* (The Society for the Study of Myth and Tradition, New York, 1981), pp. 60–73.

Calder, Jenni, *Masks of the Northwest Coast Indians* (The Royal Scottish Museum, Leaflet 7, 1983).

Crocker, J. C., 'Ceremonial Masks', *Celebration: Studies in Festivity and Ritual* (Smithsonian Institution Press, Washington, 1982).

Dooling, D. M., and Jordan-Smith, Paul (eds.), *I Become Part Of It* (Parabola Books, New York, 1989).

Duchartre, Pierre Louis, *The Italian Comedy* (Dover, New York, 1966).

Fawdry, Marguerite, *Chinese Childhood* (Pollock's Toy Theatres Ltd., London, 1977, and Seven Hills Books, Cincinnati, Ohio, 1990).

Fox, Celina and Ribeiro, Aileen, *Masquerade* (Museum of London, 1983).

Geertz, C., *The Interpretation of Cultures* (Hutchinson, London, 1975, and Basic Books, New York, 1977).

Gill, Sam, 'It's Where You Put Your Eyes', in Dooling, D.M., and Jordan-Smith, Paul (eds.), *I Become Part of It* (Parabola Books, New York, 1989), pp. 75–87.

Goonatilleka, M. H., *Masks of Sri Lanka* (Department of Cultural Affairs, Sri Lanka, 1976).

Goonatilleka, M. H., *Mask and Mask Systems of Sri*

Lanka (Tamarind Books, Colombo, Sri Lanka, 1978).

Hartnoll, Phyllis, *A Concise History of the Theatre* (Thames & Hudson, London, 1968, and New York, 1985).

Heyneman, Janet, 'Travelling Songs, Waiting Songs', in Dooling, D.M. (ed.), *Parabola, Vol. XIV, No. 1: Disciples and Discipline* (The Society for the Study of Myth & Tradition, New York, 1989), pp. 35–42.

Huxley, Francis, *The Dragon* (Thames & Hudson, London, 1979, and New York, 1988).

Jarvis, Anthea and Raine, Patricia, *Fancy Dress* (Shire Publications Ltd., Aylesbury, 1984).

Jenkins, Ian, 'Face Value: The Mask in Greece and Rome', in Mack, John (ed.), *Masks: The Art of Expression,* pp. 150–167.

Jenkins, Ron, 'Two-Way Mirrors', in Dooling, D.M. (ed.), *Parabola, Vol. VI, No. 3: Mask and Metaphor* (The Society for the Study of Myth and Tradition, New York, 1981), pp. 17–21.

Keene, Donald, *Noh: The Classical Theatre of Japan* (Kodansha International Ltd., 1966).

Kerenyi, C., 'Man and Mask', *Spiritual Disciplines: Papers from the Eranos Year Book 4* (Princeton University Press, NJ, 1985), pp. 151–167.

Lévi-Strauss, Claude, *The Way of the Masks* (Jonathan Cape, London, 1983, and University of Washington Press, 1988).

Liggett, John, *The Human Face* (Constable & Co., London, 1974).

Luthra, Chandni (ed.), 'The Folk Theatre of India', *Yatri: A Newsletter of Indian Tourism* (Department of Tourism, India, Prasad Process Ltd., Madras).

Mack, John (ed.), *Masks: The Art of Expression* (The British Museum Press, & Harry N. Abrams, New York, 1994).

Mellors, M., *et al.*, *Masks, Horniman Museum Education Centre, Teachers' Information Pack* (Greater London Education Authority, London, n.d.).

Miller, Mary Ellen, *The Art of Mesoamerica from Olmec to Aztec* (Thames & Hudson, London, & New York, 1986).

Napier, David A., *Masks, Transformation and Paradox* (University of California Press, Berkeley, 1986).

Nishikawa, Kyotaro, *Bugaku Masks* (Kodansha International Ltd., Shibundo, 1978).

Onions, C.T. (ed.), *The Shorter Oxford English Dictionary* (Oxford University Press, Oxford, 1998, and New York, 1973).

Paolozzi, Eduardo, *Lost Magic Kingdoms* (British Museum Publications, London, 1985).

Pern, Stephen, *Masked Dancers of West Africa: The Dogon* (Time-Life Books, Amsterdam, 1982).

Phillips, Tom (ed.), *Africa: The Art of a Continent* (Royal Academy of Arts, London, and Pegasus, New York, 1995).

Rawson, Philip, *Sacred Tibet* (Thames & Hudson, London, and New York, 1991).

Reeve, John, 'Multi-Cultural Work at the British Museum', *Journal of Education in Museums* No. 7 (September 1987).

Shelton, Anthony, 'Realm of the Fire Serpent', *The British Museum Society Bulletin* No. 98 (Summer 1988).

Shuel, Brian, *The National Trust Guide to Traditional Customs of Britain* (Webb & Bower, Devon, 1985).

Southern, Richard, *The Seven Ages of the Theatre* (Faber & Faber, London 1964).

Stanley, Nick, 'The Unstable Object: Reviewing the Status of Ethnographic Artefacts', *Journal of Design History, 2.2 and 3* (1989).

Steele, Philip, *Festivals Around the World* (International Picture Library, Macmillan, London, 1983).

The NCC Arts in Schools Project Team, *The Arts 5/16: Practice and Innovation* (Oliver & Boyd, Edinburgh, 1990).

Westendorf, Wolfhart, *Painting, Sculpture and Architecture of Ancient Egypt* (Harry N. Abrams, New York, & London, 1968).

Willet, Frank, *African Art* (Thames & Hudson, London, 1971, & New York, 1985).

Wosien, Maria-Gabriele, *Sacred Dance* (Thames & Hudson, London & New York, 1996).

Ziff, Trisha (ed.), *Between Worlds: Contemporary Mexican Photography* (Bellew Publishing, London, & New Amsterdam Books, Franklin, NY, 1990).

Index